"How To Invest" series

Get Smart or Get Screwed:

How To Select The Best and Get The Most From Your Financial Advisor

Paul A. Merriman

with Richard Buck

REGALO

educate - empower

Published by Regalo LLC

ISBN-13: 978-1480179530

ISBN-10: 1480179531

This publication is designed to provide accurate and authoritative information in regard to the subject matter covered. It is sold and otherwise distributed with the understanding that neither the authors nor publisher is engaged in rendering legal, accounting, securities trading or other professional services. If legal advice or other expert assistance is required, the services of a competent professional person should be sought. – *From a Declaration of Principles Jointly Adapted by a Committee of the American Bar Association and a Committee of Publishers and Associations*

To contact Regalo LLC, please email us at info@paulmerriman.com

All profits from the sale of this book – and all books in the "How To Invest" series – are donated to educational non-profit organizations. For more information, visit http://www.PaulMerriman.com

Book Design and Editorial Assistance by Aysha Griffin

Cover Design by Anne Clark

About: The "How To Invest" Series

Paul A. Merriman's "How To Invest" series, published under the Regalo imprint, provides concise and timeless information for creating a secure financial future and stress-free retirement. Each book addresses a specific audience or investor topic.

With almost 50 years of experience as a nationally recognized authority on mutual funds, asset allocation and retirement planning, Paul is committed to educating people of all ages and incomes make the most of their investments, with less risk and more peace of mind.

All profits from the sale of this series are donated to educational non-profit organizations.

The first book in the series, **FIRST-TIME INVESTOR: Grow and Protect Your Money**, gives you easy-to-understand and follow steps necessary to start, build and maintain a successful investment portfolio for life that will lead to a secure retirement. If you have ever struggled to understand how to begin investing, or you want to know that you're on the right track, this is an essential read.

This second book, **GET SMART or GET SCREWED: How To Select The Best and Get The Most From Your Financial Advisor** gives you insights into the variety of financial brokers and advisors, and the services they can – and should – offer. It includes extensive lists of questions you should ask and services you should receive from an advisor, and reasons why the brokerage industry is not serving your best interests.

To ensure that you "Get Smart," Paul helps you understand how to find and work with competent and ethical advisors, firms and products. Getting the best and most from your advisor with will save you time, grow your money, and give you peace of mind. Whether you are a first-time or savvy investor, you will learn new ways to avoid the plethora of pitfalls many investors encounter.

The third book, **101 INVESTMENT DECISIONS GUARANTEED TO CHANGE YOUR FINANCIAL FUTURE** (to be released late 2012), shows you how every decision investment decision you have – or will – make has the potential to add $1,000 or more to your wealth, and together can add up to millions of extra dollars for you and your family over the years. Presented in a well-organized workbook-style, allowing you to easily prioritize each decision, Paul Merriman explains how each decision impacts your financial future.

The "How To Invest" series books are available in paperback and eBook formats and can be purchased via **Amazon** and other outlets, or at **http://www.PaulMerriman.com**.

Acknowledgements

Over the years I have learned about investing from many wise people (and a few foolish ones as well), and I am forever indebted to them in more ways than I can say.

I would be negligent if I didn't tell you that you would not have this book in your possession without the patience and wisdom of my wife, Suzanne, and the creative, diligent work of Aysha Griffin and Richard Buck. If this book helps you, then you should be thankful that they are on my team.

Contents

INTRODUCTION

My goal in this book is to help you find – and make full use of – a top-notch financial advisor who is really *working for you*; one who will maximize the probability that you will achieve your short-term and long-term goals.

If you don't have an advisor but want or need one, this book is for you. You'll learn about three basic types of financial advisors and how to choose among them. You'll learn how to find an advisor who could become a valuable part of your life and financial success, for the rest of your life and even beyond.

If you already have an advisor, this book is also for you. You'll learn how to get the most from your relationship, as well as some of the many things your advisor can do for you. You will have the tools to know whether or not you are on the right track, and you'll feel more in control.

Since I was in the fifth grade, I've been on a diet. I tell people I've lost more than 4,000 pounds (though I will admit that I can't prove it). In 2012, while working on this book, I lost more than 20 pounds, and then put that weight back on. (Don't look to me to help you successfully lose weight!)

I've purchased almost every major diet book that has come out in the past 50 years. I've participated in more weight-loss programs and gone to more gyms than I can count. At the supermarket checkout stands I notice, as you probably have, that Cosmopolitan and other mass-circulation magazines always have new solutions to eat well, feel great and lose weight all at the same time.

All this experience has taught me a few lessons that apply to investing. For most people, losing weight is a struggle between emotional decisions driven by our subconscious minds and the iron laws of biology and physics. We humans are wired to believe that we need certain things, and this is very difficult to counteract, even when we rationally know better.

You can think of investing as a struggle between the emotions that drive us – hope, fear and greed being three prominent examples – and the iron laws of mathematics and probability.

When I'm trying to manage my weight, I do best when I find and follow a coach, trainer, or dietician. The magazines in the supermarkets, the diet books on the shelves everywhere, the exercise gyms on every street corner, and the supermarket shelves devoted to fat-free and sugar-free products: all are evidence of the huge industries that have grown up to help us with – and in some cases to exploit – our weight-loss struggles. As it turns out, the things in our best interest run counter to the interests of the multi-billion-dollar food and restaurant industries.

Investors face similar challenges. Wall Street has evolved into a gigantic industry of companies working hard to make billions of dollars getting us to make choices that – as far as I can tell – are designed more for the benefit of Wall Street than for us.

More than likely, the investment industry intersects with you personally in the form of a broker, a financial planner or an advisor of some sort.

The good news is that there are many highly qualified advisors available to meet our needs *at reasonable cost and without conflicts of interest*. The bad news is that there are also lots of advisors who operate with poor ethics and conflicts of interest.

Even the wealthiest investors who rely heavily on professionals are not entirely satisfied. Many are looking for new sources of help; some wealthy investors use multiple advisors, sometimes playing one against another.

The market research firm Cerulli Associates did a study of households with at least $10 million in investable assets. Like most of us, these households were adversely affected by the two severe bear markets of the past decade. Many of them discovered that their high-priced financial professionals didn't prevent them from suffering as much as many do-it-yourself investors were able to do for themselves.

Cerulli found that in 2012, nearly two-thirds of these very wealthy households had four or more financial advisors – that was up from about one in six in 2008. The researchers also found that 44 percent of these households fired their primary financial advisors in the wake of the 2007-2008 financial crisis.

So if the wealthiest investors can't find financial advisors worth sticking with, what makes me think that you can?

This book is my answer to that question. I'm pretty sure that the wealthy investors in that study would have been much more likely to stick with their advisors if they had followed the advice you'll find in this book – and (this is important) if they had had *reasonable expectations*.

Just as no physician can defeat the inevitability of a patient's eventual death, no financial advisor can control the financial markets and guarantee success.

Why This Book Is Different:

Why, you might ask, should you read this book instead of one of the other 6,000 or so titles available at Amazon.com that discuss investment advisors? Actually, there's no reason you shouldn't read other books on this topic. I have read many of them, and I've distilled the most important things I have learned – and I've added my own material as well.

Evaluating and using advisors is very familiar territory to me. For half a century, I've been an investor. I've been a venture capitalist. I've been a corporate officer. I've been a registered representative (broker). I've owned and managed an independent investment advisory firm. I've been an advisor to hundreds of clients. I have recruited and trained some of the best advisors in the business.

I'm totally on your side, and I have nothing to sell you and no conflict of interest. Although I have retired from the advisory firm I started, I still spend the majority of my time educating people about all aspects of investing – as I have done for many years.

I've done this at workshops, in books and articles, in podcasts, on CDs and DVDs, on the radio and on local, regional and national television. This is my life's work, and it has been for many years.

I believe the single most valuable step every investor can take is to find a competent, trustworthy advisor, even if the relationship lasts only for a year. If you find the right one (and this book tells you how), I doubt you will want to give up that advisor after a year.

A financial advisor cannot know which investments will beat the market. Nor can he build your wealth in a risk-free manner or give you access to guaranteed "deals."

However, a good advisor can and should:

• make sure you have defined your objectives in a reasonable and realistic way

• help you build a diversified, low-cost portfolio to head toward those objectives with carefully controlled risk

• help you make smart choices about mortgages, employee benefits, insurance, pensions, Social Security and leaving assets to your heirs

If this is what you want, you've found your road map here in these pages.

Before we begin that journey, I want to acknowledge that the second part of this book's title, "Get Screwed," is deliberately provocative. Before I signed off on that part of the title, I did a little research. I learned that the modern sense of the word "screw" goes back to the 17th century, when it referred to a way of "exerting pressure or coercion," probably by means of torture instruments such as thumbscrews and racks.

The non-sexual uses of the verb "screw" include getting somebody in trouble, taking advantage of somebody, cheating or robbing somebody without quite reaching into his pockets.

It seems to me that "Get Screwed" is an accurate description of what happens to many investors.

Finally, let me say a few words about how I have addressed two difficulties of writing on this topic.

Financial advice comes in many forms and from many places. Because this is a practical guide and not an academic textbook, I have had to simplify the definitions slightly of the types of investment advisors. I've lumped advisors into three categories:

      • commission based brokers
      • hourly fee-only planners
      • asset based fee-only advisors

In real life, these categories sometimes overlap and not everybody fits neatly into one of these three boxes. This book is designed to teach you how to easily find what you are looking for, regardless of anybody's title.

The English language does not make it easy to write about people of both genders. Once upon a time, it was common to use the male pronouns to refer to all adults. Fortunately, women are now professionals in almost all fields, and certainly there are many fine female financial advisors. In fact, the first advisor I ever hired for our firm (except for my son) was a woman, and she's still taking tremendously good care of many clients.

In writing about brokers and other advisers I could have resorted to using phrases like "he or she" and "him or her." However, this is unnecessarily awkward, and I have reverted to the old practice of using the male pronouns. As you read these pages you might conclude that I think all advisors are men. That's not the case at all, and I'm pointing it out here so you will know.

The first half of this book is your practical guide to finding and working with the right broker for you. The second half was originally conceived as a project with a working title of "101 reasons I Don't Trust Brokers." However, after a while, I realized that that provocative topic is much better treated as part of a practical book.

In my view, this book will be a success if it helps you to hire the right financial help *in order to achieve your objectives*. Anything less could subject you to potentially catastrophic consequences. Ultimately, you are the one who will make the choice. I hope you'll choose an advisor who is ethical and competent. I hope you'll choose a firm that's ethical and competent. I hope you will invest in low-cost, tax-efficient products that have the best combination of expected returns and risks.

If you do those things, I think you will Get Smart, and you won't Get Screwed.

Paul Merriman

BOOK I:
Get Smart

Part 1:
The lay of the land

Chapter 1: What kind of advisor do you have?

Most people have a primary source for their investment advice and ideas, whether it's a friend or relative, a newspaper or online columnist, a stockbroker or banker or planner. But, I believe, too many people are far too casual about where they turn for advice. Many investors have no clear idea what type of advisor they have.

If you have a medical condition that needs attention, you'll choose a practitioner carefully. You would not expect a heart surgeon to take care of an eye infection, for example; nor would you rely on a pediatrician to take care of your aging parents. This is so obvious that it's almost funny. But millions of investors make fuzzy decisions like that when they choose a professional to take care of them financially.

In this chapter I'll introduce you to the most important broad-brush differences among financial advisors in order to help you sort out your options and determine what type of advisor will be best for you. In a later chapter, I'll give you a more detailed road map for choosing.

In talking to thousands of investors over many years, I have come to believe that most people choose their financial advisors on the basis of friendships, affiliations (somebody from the same church or club, for example) or recommendations from people they know.

This method of choosing an advisor is easy. And it produces comfort, which is highly valued in our society. But comfort and competence don't always come in the same package. And they don't have anything to do with friendship. In fact, the opposite could be true. If you ever decide you need to fire or replace your advisor, it will be much easier if your relationship is purely professional, and not based on a familial or friendly association.

When your financial future is at stake, you are going to be far better off if your decisions are based on competence than if they're based only on the advice of somebody who was easy to choose.

In order to "Get Smart" about your finances, you may have to resist taking the easiest path. You may need to do some careful thinking about what you want to accomplish and on whom you will rely.
This book is designed to help you do that careful thinking so you can make the choices that are most likely to lead to your long-term success. So let's roll up our sleeves and wade into this topic.

Once upon a time, when life was simpler, a family's financial advisor was likely to be a stockbroker. Often this role was shared by a life insurance salesman, and sometimes by a banker as well.

But now there are dozens if not hundreds of designations held by professionals who want to help us with our financial lives. There are Certified Financial Planners, Certified Public Accountants, registered representatives, financial planners, financial consultants, wealth management consultants... this list could go on and on.

A lot of these people carry impressive titles like vice president; but sometimes a title like that indicates little more than somebody's ability to sell financial products.

Many brokerage houses, hoping to win the confidence of clients, infuse their brokers with puffed-up credentials that are mostly meaningless. Sometimes they tell outright lies, though rarely in writing. Upon learning that someone is a "financial planner," a prospective client may assume a level of expertise. But often, all that's required to legally call yourself a financial planner is to file some registration forms with your state's securities regulators.

Some advisors falsely state or imply that they are Certified Financial Planners, invoking a prestigious designation that can be obtained only by rigorous education and must pass not only a background check but work for at least three years under the tutelage of experienced CFPs.

According to one study, only about one out of five "financial planners" is a Certified Financial Planner. Many would-be CFPs have fulfilled only some of the requirements for that designation, but some of them still represent themselves to the public as Certified Financial Planners.

You could spend a good deal of time and study trying to understand all these titles and designations. Fortunately, I don't think that's necessary. In fact, there are only two absolutely critical distinctions that should separate who is on your list of candidates and who is not. I'm going to cover these in the next two chapters, but here's a brief preview:

- First, some advisors have a strict legal responsibility to you, while others can fudge all sorts of things for their own benefit. You want the first kind.

- Second, the way that an advisor is paid matters enormously. You want one who is paid by you – and only you.

Above, I spoke of your need for competence in an advisor. This is crucial. A great deal could be written about this, and lots of people have lots of different opinions on what constitutes competence. Maybe someday I'll write a book on the subject. For now, I'll hit a few high spots.

I believe that competence is a favorable combination of *knowledge, experience and judgment*. That is what you want in an advisor.

You can get the first two of these qualities, knowledge and experience, if you work with a Certified Financial Planner. (I am not a CFP myself nor do I have any connection with the organization that bestows that designation. My own advisor, by the way, is a CFP.)

The third attribute of competence – good judgment – is something else. It cannot be guaranteed by any private or public regulatory agency. It is not dependent on any educational degree. Over time, you will learn whether or not your advisor passed this test.

Hiring a CFP won't necessarily give you somebody with good judgment. But it will give you somebody who has pledged to abide by a strict code of ethics. And ethics, as we shall see time and again in these pages, is at the heart of finding the right advisor for you.

Chapter 2: **Legal responsibility**

Brokers and other advisors will do their best to convince you that they are on your side. Being on your side emotionally is nice. Being on your side legally is much more valuable.

Legal accountability may seem like an arcane topic, but it's extremely important. Be sure you understand this, because it is the biggest dividing line, so to speak, between the advisors you should hire and those you should not hire.

When you pay somebody for financial advice, that person has a legal responsibility to you. This legal responsibility comes in two very distinct flavors, if you will. You need to know which is which; but unfortunately you can't always tell that from job titles or designations.

For purposes of this chapter, I'm going to use the term "brokers" to describe financial professionals who have one type of responsibility and the term "registered investment advisors" to describe those who have the other.

- **Brokers** are held to a weak legal standard known as "suitability." This means the broker is required to recommend products that are "suitable" for you in light of your objectives, your income, and your age. That sounds pretty nice, but read on.

- **Registered investment advisors** are held to a much higher standard known as fiduciary responsibility. Fiduciary is a big word with a big meaning. Fiduciaries (professionals who are subject to this standard) are required to do what is *best* for their clients. They must put your interests ahead of their own and must disclose any real or potential conflicts of interest, including issues related to compensation and referrals.

To recap, a broker must recommend only products that are suitable for you, things that aren't likely to harm you. A fiduciary, on the other hand, must not only avoid harm but must do what's actually best for you.

If you were choosing a surgeon, which standard would you want to govern the person who will operate on you? Would you prefer a doctor who was required to worry only about not harming you? Or would you rather have the doctor who had to figure out, and do, what is likely to be best for you?

Here's another familiar way to grasp the difference. Imagine that you hire your sister-in-law to pick out and buy a new car for you. You tell her that you have two requirements: the car must cost less than $30,000, and it must get at least 25 miles per gallon of gas.

That would leave your sister-in-law a pretty long list of cars that would be "suitable" for you. If she were held to the "suitability" standard that applies to brokers, she could pick any car that met your two criteria. In addition, she wouldn't be under any obligation to explain to you (or anyone else) why she made the choice she did.

Now imagine that in addition to whatever you paid her for finding your new car, your sister-in-law would receive a $500 sales commission or "kickback" from the manufacturer if you bought certain makes, but no kickback if you bought other makes. Could you still rely on her to act only in your best interests when she chooses your new set of wheels?

You might wind up with an ugly, noisy car with cramped, uncomfortable seating, a model that's "on sale" because the dealer hasn't been able to find anybody who wants it. Legally, those things wouldn't matter as long as the car met your stated requirements for price and fuel economy.

You have probably shopped for cars yourself, and you know that's not how you would choose one. In addition to fuel economy and price, I'm pretty sure you would like to own a vehicle that's reliable, gives you good visibility, keeps its resale value, passes safety tests, gives you the right amount of room and has a pleasing appearance. It should fit in your garage or your driveway, too.

When you consider all those criteria, you have started to define what could be described as "the best" car for you. That's what you would look for on your own. If your sister-in-law had a **fiduciary responsibility** to you, she would need to find one that could be described as "the best" for you.

Investment products are probably much less familiar to you than cars, and in the long run the investments you own are much more important to you than the vehicles you own. *When your financial future is at stake, you shouldn't accept less than the best.*

A fiduciary is required to act in a prudent manner, with skill, diligence and care. When there's some unavoidable conflict of interest, the issue must be managed in the client's favor.

At this point you may be wondering how you can find out whether an advisor has a fiduciary duty or only the weaker "suitability" responsibility. You may be able to determine this quickly and easily by looking at the advisor's business card.

If the words "Securities offered through ..." appear on the business card, you are dealing with a broker, without fiduciary duty. If the advisor's Web site or literature makes reference to FINRA (Financial Industry Regulatory Authority) or to a "Series 7 license," you are most likely dealing with a broker.

Beyond those obvious clues, the best way to find out is simple: Just ask.

Brokers (those who do not have fiduciary responsibility) will know what to say when they hear this question. They'll have some convincing answer, and it will be your job to recognize that it really means: "No, I don't have fiduciary responsibility to my clients."

If you think an advisor is trying to fool you into thinking (incorrectly) that he has fiduciary responsibility, you can ask for it in writing. You can prepare yourself in advance with a sheet of paper ready for his signature that says:

"I, _____, affirm that I have a legally enforceable fiduciary duty to act only in the best interests of my clients, to avoid conflicts of interest wherever possible and to disclose any potential conflicts that I cannot avoid."

Even the least ethical broker, if he is licensed, will know that falsely signing such a written statement is asking for a lot of trouble in the future. No broker, and certainly no broker's supervisor, will want any such statement to turn up in a lawsuit or arbitration hearing unless it is completely true.

If your advisor won't sign such a statement, you have your answer. If you engage this person's services, you are taking risks that you don't need to take.

Most people in the investment industry know when they have a conflict of interest with investors. Many of them dislike it. Here's one example:

Early in 2012, Greg Smith wrote an article for the Opinion Page of *The New York Times* under the headline "Why I Am Leaving Goldman Sachs." After 12 years working at the firm in California, New York and London, he said he concluded that:

"The interests of the client continue to be sidelined in the way the firm operates and thinks about making money."

Smith said he was initially attracted to Goldman Sachs, one of the world's largest investment banks, because of its 143-year-old culture that earned clients' trust through teamwork, integrity "and always doing right by our clients."

"I am sad to say that I look around today and see virtually no trace of the culture that made me love working for this firm for many years," he added.

Smith said he always took "a lot of pride in advising my clients to do what I believe is right for them, even if it means less money for the firm. This view is becoming increasingly unpopular at Goldman Sachs... I attend derivatives sales meetings where not one single minute is spent asking questions about how we can help clients. It's purely about how we can make the most possible money off of them."

Goldman Sachs and many other companies have competent and intelligent advisors who would like to help. But they don't have a fiduciary responsibility to their clients. Because of that, their clients are often short-changed.

If you want to Get Smart, don't be like those clients. *Use an advisor who has a legal fiduciary responsibility to do what is best for you.*

Chapter 3: **Follow the money**

It should come as no surprise that money is the driving force behind everything that happens in the investment industry. Some naïve investors seem to think that all that matters is their own money. They often Get Screwed. Savvy investors, those who Get Smart, understand how important it is to know who pays the advisor.

When you're paying for advice (and you always pay, one way or another), there are only two basic choices:
Choice #1: You can pay your advisor, and the advisor works for you.
Choice #2: Somebody else can pay your advisor, and in effect, the advisor works for that somebody else.

Ultimately, "the boss" is the person who writes the check to pay the advisor or broker. If you are the only one who does that, then you are in charge.

You may not want to be bothered with such things. But getting this right can enrich your retirement nest egg by hundreds of thousands of dollars. How your advisor gets paid often dictates how your money is invested. And if you aren't the one in the driver's seat, look out!

Advisors who accept commissions for selling you a product have a conflict of interest. Some will try to convince you that a sales commission is no different from the annual fees that some advisors charge. But there's a world of difference, and the following true story is just one example.

I know a man named Jerry who was talked into investing $1.2 million in a variable annuity. The broker spent two hours selling this product to Jerry. The broker received a $60,000 commission. The variable annuity was technically "suitable" for Jerry, but it was far from the best way to meet his needs.

Even if such a product had been the right solution for Jerry, the broker could have recommended an annuity with much lower expenses and better investment options. However, that didn't happen because the broker would have received a much lower commission for the two hours he spent in order to make the sale.

Jerry was not the one in charge of this transaction. He didn't directly pay the $60,000 commission. The insurance company did. Jerry didn't get much value for that money. The broker did.

When you're considering hiring an advisor, you should pay a lot of attention to what it will cost you. Some of the arrangements are straightforward and others are deliberately designed to be obscure.

Don't ever forget that good advice is a valuable commodity, and you should expect to pay a fair price for it. John Bogle, the founder of The Vanguard Group and the inventor of the index fund, said it this way: "While good advice may not be cheap, bad advice always costs you dearly, no matter how little you pay for it."

There are three basic ways an advisor gets paid.

1. Commissions. This is the basic model that drives the financial industry, the real estate industry and the automobile industry. A salesperson somehow persuades a buyer to make a purchase, and a commission results. To the buyer, it always looks as if somebody else pays the commission. But it doesn't take a rocket scientist to figure out that one way or another, the only source of money from which a commission could be paid is the buyer.

If you buy a house, the seller pays the commission. That might cost the seller 6 percent of the sales price. The commission is not a secret, of course, and it's built into the asking price. Naturally, the commission is not forgotten during price negotiations.

In real estate, this isn't usually a great problem. After all, you presumably understand what a house should and should not have, you can tour the house, talk to the neighbors, bring your friends and relatives to help look it over, etc. You can probably find all the competing houses that have sold or are for sale, too.

But when you are buying a financial product like a mutual fund, the salesperson (broker or advisor) almost certainly knows much more about the products than you do. If he is paid a commission, he first of all wants you to buy something, and he understandably prefers it to be something that pays a larger commission instead of a smaller one.

You know how to recognize a good house or a good car for yourself. But when you're shopping for a mutual fund, your advisor almost always has superior knowledge with which to steer you to make the "right" choice, one that will generate an attractive commission.

In Book II, I'll show you many examples of how this conflict of interest plays out. For now, I'll just say that while a commission-based advisor may seem cheap, the opposite is often the case.

2. Hourly fees. Many advisors avoid the conflict of interest that I just described by accepting no commissions at all, instead charging you for their services by the hour. Some will charge a flat fee for making an overall plan and recommendations. This usually means you'll buy no-load mutual funds, ones that don't pay commissions. This is good, because no-load funds usually have lower expenses, leaving a higher percentage of their portfolio returns in your account. The result is better performance.

Some hourly advisors operate under an agreement in which any commission they are paid is credited to you against your fee. For example, if you buy an insurance policy recommended by the advisor, the fee you pay the advisor is reduced by whatever commission is paid to the advisor. This removes any incentive the advisor might have to recommend one policy over another because of a commission. Instead, the choice can be made entirely on the basis of what is best for you.

Hourly advisors thus avoid most of the problems that plague the clients of commission-based brokers. Still, this payment method has a few drawbacks.

An advisor who charges by the hour earns more if he spends more time on your behalf. If your situation requires only one hour of work, you may be charged for only that hour. This may not even begin to compensate the advisor for the time (and maybe money) he spent to acquire you as a client and keep records of what you did. So your advisor may be tempted to find more things to do, in order to increase his billable hours. This isn't necessarily in your best interest.

A more subtle drawback is that you, as a client, may be reluctant to "buy" the time of your advisor to address issues that you think you can figure out on your own. Your own frugality may thus prevent you from getting the full benefits of having an advisor.

In fact, your advisor probably can do much more for you than you initially sought. I'll discuss this more in a later chapter.

3. Asset-based fee. Many advisors charge you based on the assets that they manage for you. For many investors, I think this is usually the best arrangement.

A typical scenario might work like this: Your portfolio is worth $1 million, and your advisor charges 1 percent per year to take care of all your needs. That means you pay $10,000 a year. The advisor's incentive is to keep your assets from shrinking and, if possible within the amount of risk you should be taking, to also make your money grow. That's exactly what you too should want.

Your asset-based advisor won't be driven by the incentive of earning sales commissions. He wants you to have low-cost, efficient investments that will keep as much money as possible in your pocket.

His services are not limited in the time he can spend with you, and in the best of circumstances he is free to give you many services, as I will describe in Chapter 7. If you're paying 1 percent a year for somebody to manage your money, you should get those services as part of the deal.

Asset-based advisors may not want to talk about the inherent fairness of requiring somebody with $800,000 in assets to pay twice as much for financial help as somebody with $400,000. It certainly does not cost the advisor twice as much, on average, to take care of the former client as it does to take care of the latter one. Clients with more money under management may in effect be subsidizing clients who have less.

To some extent this is just the way the system works. For example, mutual fund shareholders are in the same boat. Annual fund expenses are calculated as a percentage of assets, and those with higher balances bear more of the costs.

Many asset-based managers overcome this to some extent by means of tiered rates for larger accounts. They may charge one percentage for money up to $1 million and a lower rate for balances above that.

Having an asset-based advisor is not entirely free from conflicts of interest. If you are considering using a big chunk of your portfolio to pay off your mortgage, your advisor might be reluctant to recommend that course of action because it would reduce his fee.

However, a good advisor should be able to discuss this with you frankly. If your advisor wants to keep your business and have you refer other business to him, he will want to do everything he can to make sure your total financial situation is in the best possible shape.

That, it turns out, is exactly what you too should want.

Part 2:
How advisors typically work

Chapter 4: If your advisor is paid by commissions

There are many competent, ethical brokers who help their clients through all sorts of situations. Brokers make millions of financial transactions happen every business day. If the brokers were suddenly gone, the system could collapse in a hurry. At one time or another, almost every investor uses the services of a broker, and in this chapter I want to give you a brief look at how such a relationship typically works.

A broker's most basic job is to facilitate a transaction by bringing together a buyer and a seller. If you want to buy 100 shares of Apple stock, a broker can make it happen quickly and easily; his firm may sell the stock directly to you or may locate an investor who owns the shares and is ready to sell them.

In practice, such routine transactions are almost completely automated, and a broker doesn't have to search for a buyer or seller. If you wanted to buy (or sell) 10 million shares of Apple stock, it would be another matter, of course.

In Book II, you'll learn about dozens of ways commission-based advisors – here I will refer to them simply as brokers – take what I believe is unfair advantage of their clients. Among the three types of advisory relationship I have outlined, I believe you are likely to be least-well-served by having a broker.

There are three main varieties of brokerage firms:

1. Traditional "full-service" firm like Merrill Lynch.
2. Discount firm like Charles Schwab, Fidelity and Vanguard.
3. Deep-discount firms that primarily do business over the Internet. Scottrade is one example.

At Merrill Lynch and similar firms, you'll pay the highest commission rates, and you'll have the widest range of services available. You will be assigned to a broker, most likely somebody with a title such as financial consultant or vice president. Your broker will have access to his firm's proprietary research as well as to a full range of products available to address whatever needs you might have.

At a discount brokerage firm, such as Charles Schwab, you will also probably be assigned to a broker, and you'll probably pay lower commission rates on the trades you make. You may have access to independent research reports on companies and funds you're considering.

At a deep-discount firm such as Scottrade, you will pay the lowest commission rates. Although on paper a broker may be assigned to you, you will be mostly on your own, with online resources, and free of the sales pressure that I describe in Book II. Often, you will be granted a certain number of commission-free online trades.

Commission-free trades may seem like an incredibly good deal, but they aren't if they tempt you to do much more buying and selling than you should

Opening a brokerage account is designed to be easy, and sometimes you can do most or all of it online. At many firms, once your account is open you can buy and sell without the advice of a broker. At a full-service firm you will likely be invited to meet in person or over the phone with a broker who will want to get to know you and your financial situation.

This broker's financial incentive is to get you to buy and sell. Some brokers are pushy about this, while others are relatively laid back. Unless you have a large amount of money, you're likely to be assigned to a relatively new broker who is trying hard to build a book of business, and who is under considerable pressure to generate commission income.

Whatever stocks, bonds or mutual funds you buy through a broker will usually be held in what's called "street name." If you really want a certificate showing that you own those 100 shares of Apple stock, you can get it, but there may be an extra charge. Usually, the brokerage firm keeps the title to the assets in electronic form, although they are assigned to you and owned by you.

This arrangement is convenient and efficient, and (not quite by accident) it makes it easy for you to buy and sell more often and more quickly than if you took actual possession of stock and bond certificates.

The experience you have with a broker can vary widely. In the ideal case, you are assigned to somebody with lots of experience and enough business that he has no need to pressure you to make trades. He may have time and expertise to help you with all your financial needs.

However, even the best broker must still earn a living. Even if he concludes that the best thing for you is to keep your money in the bank, he cannot afford to make such a recommendation because it will generate no income for him or his firm. He will always, therefore, have some alternative course of action to suggest, one that will produce commission income in one form or another.

Every broker has access to no-load mutual funds, and many brokers can help you buy such funds and charge you a small commission. However, they aren't likely to volunteer this information. Early in his career, every broker is taught how easy it is to tout the "benefits" of funds that pay brokerage commissions.

If you know what you want to do and are comfortable with making trades online, I think your best bet is to use a discount brokerage firm like Scottrade. Resist the temptation to indulge in all the commission-free trades you may be offered. Here, your greatest risk is overconfidence and thinking you know more than you do.

If you need the services of a personal broker, your greatest risk is being manipulated into making trades and decisions that are primarily aimed at generating income for the firm – and only secondarily aimed at bringing some benefit to you.

Most brokers recommend that their clients invest in stocks and mutual funds. A typical broker may spend most of his working hours talking about stocks, which ones are going up, which are going down, and so forth. But not all those brokers put their money where their mouths are.

A well-known stockbroker in Seattle (his live stock-market commentaries were on the radio every business day) once told a newspaper reporter that he didn't own any stocks himself. His money, he said, was invested in real estate.

In Book II you'll find dozens of examples of how some brokers take advantage of their clients. Here are three:

1. **Churning**: Churning is a practice that happens when brokers try to generate unnecessary buying and selling activity in a client's account, primarily to earn commissions.

Most of the time, investors are served best when they buy carefully chosen securities and then hold them for the long run. But this does not generate commissions. Churning does, and it's an easily understood example of a conflict of interest between the brokerage firm and the client.

Your broker will never talk to you about "churning," but this practice is alive and well. Informally, churning is measured in what brokers refer to among themselves as a "spin ratio." If a broker's total assets under management total $10 million, and if his clients' sales and purchases in a year total $4 million, he is said to have a spin ratio of 40 percent.

Some brokers have been known to have ratios over 100 percent. As long as they avoid legal trouble for their firms, these brokers tend to be quite popular among their bosses because of the income they generate.

I hope you will not underestimate how serious this practice can be. In September 2012, Investmentnews.com reported that the Securities and Exchange Commission had charged three former brokers of an Atlanta investment firm, JP Turner & Co., with managing seven clients' accounts with turnover rates so high that the underlying investments would have had to achieve returns of more than 73 percent in order to just break even.

During 2008 and 2009, when most investors were suffering through a severe bear market, the SEC said, JP Turner charged these seven investors $845,000 in commissions and fees while the clients – who had specified they wanted conservative investments with low risks – lost $2.7 million. JP Turner, by the way, has brokers in more than 200 U.S. offices, according to Investmentnews.com.

2. **Emotional appeal**: Brokers are trained to overcome virtually all objections and appeal to emotions in order to generate sales. When they are under pressure to sell some particular product, brokers learn to emphasize to clients how much trust other investors (who of course are non-experts) have placed in that product.

If you are on the receiving end of such a pitch, you might hear something like: "I like this (stock, fund, annuity, whatever) so much that I have put my own mother's money into it." (Of course, you'll never be shown the broker's mother's account statement to verify this; and even if it were true, does this mean anything?)

Years ago when I was still a bit naïve, I personally got snookered by a variation of this appeal. A particular investment was described to me this way: "This is a sure thing. In fact, Jack Sikma (at that time an all-star center for the Seattle Supersonics) is putting his money into it."

Only later did I see through this nonsensical implied endorsement, which of course was never documented. Jack Sikma was indeed a wonderful basketball player. But I was somehow expected to believe that made him a great judge of investments.

Bernie Madoff's notorious scam spread like wildfire partly because so many investors believed, correctly or not, that other people they admired or knew were putting money into it.

3. **Trust**. For my third example, I turn to an assumption that many investors make about the advisors they trust. You might think that a broker who treats you as a friend and valuable client would want to discourage you from doing things that are obviously likely to fail. I'm talking about the "great ideas" that you yourself bring up for discussion. Example: "Hey, I read about this great (fill in the blank) that's paying a dividend and could double in the next year. I'd like to get some."

A truly ethical broker might try to prevent you from doing that. But in the real world, the broker has a customer who wants to buy something, and that means a customer who wants to generate a commission. That is a very hard thing for any broker to resist.

And what if the broker knows your idea is a very unwise proposition? He won't want to leave a door open for any regulators to accuse him and the firm of recommending an unwise investment.

The solution is easy. The broker simply writes "unsolicited" on the order form. To everyone who knows the inside code of Wall Street, understands that means: "I didn't tell the client to do this. It was his idea."

I have a friend who worked for a large brokerage firm. He said his colleagues loved clients who wanted to actively trade commodities and volatile stocks. Even though the brokers knew it would probably end badly, in the meantime their clients generated lots of easy commissions.

That gives you a little taste of the bad news about brokers. Fortunately, there is good news. You have a choice, and you can do business with advisors who don't have such sales incentives.

In the next chapter, we'll discuss working with an advisor who charges clients by the hour.

Chapter 5: If your advisor charges by the hour

In some ways, having a relationship with a fee-based advisor can be the Gold Standard of getting financial help. This is particularly true if your advisor is competent and ethical – and even better if he has a fiduciary responsibility to you.

When you pay somebody an hourly fee for help, it doesn't matter how much money you have. It doesn't matter whether you're just starting out or a veteran investor. It doesn't matter whether you know next to nothing or you know a great deal.

You could think of this arrangement as "a la carte" help in which you pay for only what you want and need. An hourly-fee advisor can discuss costs up-front so you know in advance how much you're likely to pay. Usually you will have a written contract that spells out the scope of work to be done and the charges for it.

If your needs are relatively simple, your hourly cost could also be relatively small. If you need guidance with an array of complex issues, you'll pay more. You can hire one advisor to help you with some areas and another advisor to help in other areas. (However, even when you have a "team" of advisors, it's very helpful to have one person with an overview of your full situation – someone you can think of as the quarterback.)

In contrast to a broker, who is incentivized to focus on selling you financial products, a fee-only advisor can afford to do much more for you. If you like, you can hire him to help you set short-term and long-term goals, determine how much risk you should take with your investments, plan for your retirement and figure out how your family might be taken care of if you were to die prematurely.

You can ask for a comprehensive written financial plan and get help, whenever you need it, with taxes, insurance, your mortgage and other debts, funding college education, estate planning, employee benefits and retirement issues such as pensions and Social Security.

There are many sources of hourly financial help, and I think one of the best places to start looking is the Garrett Planning Network.

This network, founded in 2000 by Sheryl Garrett, a Certified Financial Planner, is made up of several hundred independent advisors and planners throughout the United States. They don't accept sales commissions, and most of them use Vanguard's low-cost no-load mutual funds.

Garrett advisors are Certified Financial Planners or actively working toward achieving that designation. To remain in the network, they must comply with all state and federal regulations that govern financial advisors and stick to a code of ethics.

These fee-only advisors are able to help a broad cross-section of individuals and families of all ages. If you're a do-it-yourself type, you may really appreciate being able to buy just the help you want when you need it.

An hourly advisor can be a good source of objective advice if much, or all, of your portfolio is in an employer retirement plan such as a 401(k). A commissioned salesperson may not be able to sell products inside such an account, and an asset-based manager may not be able to manage it. Your employer may be severely restricted by law in the advice it can give you. But an hourly advisor can help you get the most benefit from the investment options available in the plan and then periodically review your portfolio to keep it properly balanced.

Paying for financial advice by the hour is likely to cost you less than paying for it through commissions on products or (at least if you have substantial assets) paying on the basis of the investment assets you own.

The hourly fee arrangement lets you periodically ask your advisor if a particular piece of work to be done is likely to be worth the amount of time you'll have to pay for. A good advisor should be happy to discuss this with you and happy to do only the most productive tasks.

While an hourly planner can be great for many people, this arrangement isn't for everybody. If your finances are complex and involve restricted stocks and trusts, you probably will do better by hiring a planner to manage your assets and charge on that basis. That arrangement is the topic of the following chapter.

Chapter 6: **If you have an asset-based advisor**

In many ways, having a relationship with an asset-based advisor can be the Gold Standard of getting financial help. This is particularly true if you have a competent, ethical advisor who has a fiduciary responsibility to you and is readily available to you.

Before you open such an account, you'll typically be invited to a series of meetings in which you and the advisor determine whether you are a good fit for one another. These meetings can take place in person, over the phone or, increasingly, online. If you're married or in a committed relationship, your spouse or partner will usually be included.

One critical point will be the amount of money you have available to invest. Advisory firms will usually open accounts only when they meet a minimum size set by the firm. These minimums can be as low as $100,000 or as high as $10 million. Minimums of $500,000 to $1 million are common.

Typically, asset-based advisory firms charge 1 to 2 percent per year of the assets they manage for clients. Often, the fee is cut in half for balances over $1 million. Further cuts may apply to larger balances, for instance those over $5 million or $10 million.

Your advisor will want you to understand at least the basics of his – and his firm's – investment philosophy. You should take whatever time is necessary to absorb this information. Use the topics in Chapter 7 to fill in the blanks of this discussion, and don't hesitate to ask as many questions as you need to. If you become a client, you will be asked to buy into the firm's market approach, and you'll be expected to "stick with the program" when things get uncomfortable in the market, which they inevitably will. So make sure you understand that program.

In contrast to the commission-based advisor, who wants to generate transactions, and the hourly fee advisor who wants the clock to start running, your asset-based advisor will typically spend more time with you up-front.

If there's any pressure from such an advisor, it may be to bring more of your assets under his umbrella. From his point of view, managing most or all of your investment assets will mean a bigger base on which to compute your fee, with little or no additional cost to the advisor.

Many investors are reluctant to bring more assets under the management of their advisor, believing they can get everything they need by meeting only the advisor's minimum balance requirement.

However, I can think of three potential benefits you will get by bringing your whole portfolio under your advisor's umbrella:

1. This will make your life simpler, with fewer accounts to track.
2. It will help your advisor take a big-picture approach to your finances and make periodic rebalancing easier.
3. If you have chosen an advisor with a low-cost investment approach you like, you may have better investments than you could get on your own.

In the end, only you can weigh the costs against the benefits.

The initial time you and your advisor spend in building the relationship represents a significant commitment on the part of your advisor and the firm for which he works. If you use this time well, it should be mutually beneficial.

The more your advisor knows about you, the more help he can be. One important topic you will cover is investment risk, and specifically how much risk you are able and willing to take. The result of these conversations will be a decision on your overall asset allocation, typically how much of your money should be held in cash, how much in bonds, and how much in stocks.

At some point you will be asked to sign papers that will let the advisory firm manage your investments. You may need to consolidate multiple accounts in the care of a new custodial account at a discount brokerage, such as Charles Schwab.

In one common arrangement, your advisory firm never takes actual possession of your assets, which remain registered in your name. What you'll sign is a limited trading authorization so the advisor can make trades and, if you have authorized it, deduct money from your accounts to pay your advisory fees.

You'll typically receive regular statements from the brokerage firm and separate account statements from your advisor. This gives you an easy way to cross-check the numbers to make sure the advisor and the brokerage firm agree on your balances.

Some asset-based advisors may want to put most or all of your money in individual stocks or bonds, but I recommend you steer clear of that. As I have said many times, I believe you will be much better served by investing in mutual funds than in individual stocks. And make sure they are no-load funds.

So far I have described the mechanics of establishing the account or accounts that will get your money under management. The really good stuff starts after that, the services you can get from an asset-based advisor without paying extra. You'll find a list of such things in Chapter 9. This is why it can be worthwhile to pay that 1 percent annual fee (or whatever the percentage is).

Although a much more complete list is in Chapter 9, I'll give you two examples of what an advisor can do that you might not realize.

Example One: I know a client of one fee-based advisor who had a very brief window of time to decide what to do about some stock options in the company she worked for. The whole topic was far beyond her comfort level. Fortunately, her advisor was familiar with stock options. Because he also was familiar with her whole situation, he could quickly sort through the choices she had and make a recommendation. She later reported that his advice saved her from losing nearly $300,000.

Example Two: Here's another case that demonstrates the value of having a good advisory firm on your side. The story involves a client whom I will call Lucky. This account was held in Lucky's name at a custodial brokerage firm. At that firm, a clerk mistakenly deposited $20,000 into Lucky's account. This money belonged to some other investor, who didn't notice that it was missing for about eight months. During that time, stocks were in a major bull market, and Lucky's account earned about $7,500. When the error was discovered, the custodian (as it should have) removed the $20,000 from Lucky's account and restored it to its rightful owner. The custodian also wanted to take back most of the $7,500 of gains that had been earned in Lucky's account.

Fortunately for Lucky, the client services team at his advisory firm persuaded the custodian to let Lucky keep the entire $7,500. Lucky certainly could not have accomplished that on his own. Whatever he paid his advisor for managing that account, I think Lucky certainly got his money's worth.

If you can find an advisor and an advisory firm that does things like this for its clients, you may be in luck yourself.

Part 3:
How to choose the right advisor for you

Chapter 7: What to ask before you hire an advisor

Every year, millions of investors get poor financial advice from people whom they pay and trust. In part, they have themselves to blame. It's been said many times that most people spend more time and thought planning their annual vacation than taking care of their financial future.

It's easy – too easy, actually – to casually choose a financial advisor on the basis of a referral from somebody you know or something you read, or just because the advisor is somebody you happened to meet.

In my opinion, investors who pick their advisors very carefully almost always wind up with better outcomes than those who pick casually and uncritically. If you're shopping for an advisor, one of the best ways you can spend half an hour is thinking ahead of time about the best questions to ask.

In this chapter I'll give you a list of things to ask a prospective advisor. You can also use these as topics to discuss if you already have an advisor.

Most advisors will gladly meet with prospective clients for a free introductory session so that both parties can find out if there's a good mutual fit. You can be sure the advisor will have a clear idea of what he wants to accomplish in such a meeting. You'll be asked a lot of questions about yourself, your goals and needs and your experience with investing.

I think you should know what you want to accomplish as well. The list in this chapter will help you do that. You probably won't ask every question on my list, but at the very least you should read them over in advance so you know the general lay of the land.

A good place to start is to ask is for an overview of the process the advisor will go through to determine whether or not you are a good fit for him and his firm, and whether he believes that he is the right person to take care of you.

That discussion may uncover quite a bit of the information in the following list of questions. Then you can use these questions to make sure you have touched on the most important topics.

Some questions below refer to topics that are outside the scope of this book. If you don't recognize some of the terms (such as Form ADV or tax-loss harvesting) I suggest you do a search on Investopedia for background information. Even if you don't understand the issues, the questions are worth asking. You could say something like: "What do I need to know about _____?" and see where the conversation leads. This will give you a good opportunity to test this advisor's willingness and ability to educate you in a way that leads you to trust him.

1. Questions about the firm for which your advisor works:

- How long has your firm been in business?
- How many clients do you personally have?
- How many clients does your firm have?
- How much money do you personally have under management?
- How much money does your firm have under management?
- Who owns your company?
- What does your company do in order to attract new business?

- How would you describe your ideal client?
- When your company is recruiting financial advisors, what process do you use? What are the most important qualifications?
- Will you give me contact information for a few clients who know your firm well?
- Do you require your clients to give you a limited or general power of attorney?
- Will you give me a copy of your Form ADV and go through it with me to help me understand it?
- Do you have a way to measure the value your clients receive in relationship to the fees they pay?

3. The specific advisor with whom you would work.

- How long have you been working at this firm, and why did you choose this firm to work for?

- Are you a Certified Financial Planner?

- Please tell me about your background, training and experience.

- Do you and the other advisors in your firm work as individuals or as part of a team? If you are a team, please describe how that works.

- If I found that our personalities were not a good match, would I be able to switch to a different advisor within your firm?

4. Investments

- Please describe your firm's investment philosophy and your personal investment philosophy.

- What types of products do you recommend for clients, and why have you chosen them?

- If I became a client, how would you go about determining my tolerance for risk?

- How would you translate my risk tolerance into the appropriate asset allocation for me?

- How would you determine what investment strategy is right for me?

- Do you provide your clients with continuing access to relevant academic research?

- Do you provide any source of continuing education for your clients?

- How do you make sure that you are keeping up to date in your field?

- **5. Service**

- If I became a client, how often would we be likely to meet?

- What topics could I expect to come up in regular meetings?

- Would you want to meet regularly with my spouse (or partner) as well as with me personally?

- What is the most common way you communicate with your clients? Email? Phone? Postal mail? In-person meetings?

- How long do clients usually have to wait for a response when they ask a question via a phone call or email?

- What is the scope of financial help that you give to clients?

- If my advisor were unavailable for any reason, who would be available to help me? How would this person know my needs, wishes, risk tolerance and objectives?

- How often does your firm rebalance clients' portfolios? Do you have a process in place to avoid or minimize any unfavorable tax consequences from rebalancing?

- Do you routinely look for tax-loss-harvesting opportunities?

- Do your advisors offer help to your clients' children, grandchildren or other family members without extra charge?

- Are your clients' investments held in your firm's "street name" or in the clients' names? What firm do you use as a custodian, and why did you choose it?

- How often do your clients receive regular statements?

- Do the statements include a client's recent and long-term returns?

- Can your clients check their balances online?

- How do you help your clients stick to their strategies during discouraging market periods?

- What is your firm's retention rate for clients?

By the time you cover this list of topics, you will have learned a great deal about a firm and an advisor you are considering. And if you go through the same list with two or three firms, you will find it easy to compare and contrast them on the important points that apply to you.

This will make you a good shopper and help you to Get Smart.

Chapter 8: Finding the ideal financial advisor

It's not hard to find articles online about how to choose a good financial planner. Much of that advice is similar to what you will find in this book.

Writers often suggest asking for references from people you know and searching online databases such as the National Association of Personal Financial Advisors, the Alliance of Cambridge Advisors and the American Institute of Certified Public Accountants. (When you are considering a CPA, see if you can find one who has earned the designation of Personal Financial Specialist.)

You may want to ask for a reference from another professional. You'll be told to understand how a planner is paid and do a background check. These are all good suggestions.

To do a background check on a specific advisor or broker, I suggest a couple of useful online resources. One is from a non-government agency, and the second is from the Securities and Exchange Commission. *Forbes* magazine wrote a good article on this (July 5, 2011).

In this chapter, I want to give you my own perspective on this whole topic. I believe you can and should do better than just finding a good advisor. I believe you can find one who could be described as "the best" advisor.

When I put myself in the shoes of a client, I view the ideal advisor as somebody who:

- believes in building properly diversified investment portfolios based on academic research, not on sales pitches and hype from Wall Street.
- is a Certified Financial Planner or has equivalent knowledge.
- accepts no commissions and gets all his income from client fees.
- has fiduciary responsibility to me.
- has access to a network of other professionals to help me with taxes, estate planning, insurance, legal matters and so forth.

- is available to me by phone or email on short notice if necessary.
- takes the time to get to know me as thoroughly as possible.
- treats my time and money with respect, as if I were his most important client.
- is somebody I like and look forward to talking to.

In addition to all that, I believe the ideal advisor works for an ideal firm.

Such a firm has:

- many advisors who share the same investment philosophy and operate as a team, so that clients are never forced to wait long for help.
- access to Dimensional Fund Advisors asset-class funds, which in my view are the best in the business.
- a research staff committed to finding every possible way to improve clients' returns and control the risk to which those clients are exposed.
- a team of people to help with paperwork, tax documentation and the many other essential details that usually do not require the direct involvement of financial advisors.
- a clean record with state and federal regulatory agencies.
- no history of major legal complaints filed by clients.
- been in business for at least a decade, manages at least $500 million and has at least 500 clients.

I can all but guarantee that you won't find an advisory firm like that by accepting cold calls, responding to direct mail solicitations or Internet advertisements or by accepting offers of free meals combined with seminars.

So where can you find the advisory firm that I'm recommending? I think almost every major U.S. city has one or more such firms that will serve clients who have at least $500,000 or $1 million to invest.

If I were trying to find such a firm, I would contact Dimensional Fund Advisors to be referred to firms in my area that make the grade. If you follow this link, I encourage you to browse through the DFA site, as it contains a lot of useful information that's beyond what I can present in this book.

*   *   *

In the final analysis, you are the boss, and the advisor is your employee. You'll get the most from this relationship if you remember to do two things: Hire carefully, and be a good boss.

Part 4:
How to get the most from your advisor

Chapter 9: What you can and should get from an advisor

Financial advice isn't free. One way or another, if you have a financial advisor, you will pay. It's up to you to make sure you get your money's worth. If you choose your advisor very carefully and use him well, you are likely to get far more than your money's worth.

In this chapter, I'll tell you what that could mean. I'll tell you some things you should expect from any advisor you hire. And I'll give you a list of some of the many services you can get from a good advisor. You won't need all of them, but you may want or need more of them than you think right now.

.I feel strongly that virtually every investor should work with a professional advisor for at least one year. All the services I list in this chapter are available, but no advisor can do everything in a week or two.

Most of the biggest financial decisions in your life can be made within one year, although you probably will need to revisit various issues from time to time as your life evolves and your circumstances change.

I believe you should find an advisor with whom you are willing to commit to working for at least a full year. The time you spend choosing such an advisor will be worthwhile. (If you have an immediate need for something specific, an hourly planner can help you.)

In one year with an advisor, you'll have plenty of opportunity to see if this person is someone you want to work with permanently, for the rest of your life.

Personally, I have an advisor who is likely to outlive me by 30 years. I expect him to continue working for me, and my family, for as long as I live; that way I won't have to switch to a different advisor or a different firm.

I have spent enough time with my advisor for us to know each other well. I don't have to worry about my investments, because I can count on him to do whatever worrying is necessary (very little, as it turns out, because he and I have carefully positioned my portfolio to withstand anything that's likely to happen).
This may seem strange to you: I really don't want to spend more time and energy thinking about my investments. I've done that very thoroughly, and now my job is to live life. I want to read and write books. I want to travel, play golf and go to concerts. I want to walk on the beach and attend interesting lectures. I want to talk politics with interesting people, and especially I want to spend time with my family and friends.

With all that life offers me, why would I want to spend my time worrying about my investments? Fortunately, I have found somebody who is not only qualified to do that, but somebody who actually enjoys doing it. He is my advisor.

I hope you can obtain that level of confidence in an advisor. If you choose carefully and work with somebody for a year, you'll know. As you work with your advisor during this year, think about the following list of attributes. I believe you should be able to take them for granted from any advisor you hire.

1. Your advisor should be truthful and honest with you at all times.
2. Your advisor should actively earn your full trust, not just assume that he has it.
3. Your advisor should conduct himself in a manner that makes you feel comfortable opening up to him and telling him everything.
4. Your advisor should be somebody who can win the trust and confidence of your spouse or partner.
5. Your advisor should treat you, your time and your goals with respect.

6. Your advisor should be willing to answer your questions on any financial topic.
7. Your advisor should be comfortable acknowledging when he doesn't know something, and should be willing and able to work with you to get the answers and help that you need. He shouldn't ever feel the need to make up an answer he doesn't know.
8. Your advisor should listen to you and treat your fears, your desires and your questions seriously.
9. Your advisor should treat your confidential information as such and should not divulge confidential information about other clients to you.
10. Your advisor should give you his full attention when you're talking or meeting.
11. Your advisor should accept your calls even if you don't have more money to invest.
12. When your advisor makes a mistake, he should inform you as soon as possible and offer to make things right for you.
13. Your advisor should make sure you have a competent backup advisor for times when he is unavailable. He should make sure this other advisor has full access to your records.

Those items will set the tone of the relationship you have with your advisor. They will color all the advice and service you get. Now let's look at some of the many services you can get from a good advisor.

I have not listed these in any particular order. Some will apply to you, and others won't. The most important one for you may be in the middle or toward the end of the list.

If you're shopping for an advisor, keep shopping until you find one who will provide you with all you need or want from the following list.

Your advisor should help you allocate your investments among stocks, bonds and cash. Within each of those categories he should help you find the right mix of asset classes. In bonds, that means short-term vs. medium term vs. long term, and government vs. corporate. In stocks, that means making sure you have the right mix of large-cap, small-cap, U.S. and international funds, value and growth funds.

Your advisor should give you one or more tests to determine your tolerance for risk. He should discuss the results with you and explain what they mean in relation to the proper asset allocation of your portfolio.

Your advisor should always be looking for low-cost ways to achieve your objectives and should minimize the expenses you will inevitably pay when you invest.

Your advisor should be able to gather all the information on your finances and help you see the big picture in perspective, perhaps giving you insights you have not had before.

If you have children (or other relatives) or charities that seem to always want money from you, your advisor should help you learn how to respond to them. I once had a client who used me as a way to say no to her daughter's requests for money.

Your advisor should create a relationship with your spouse, your partner or your grown children so he can help them after your death. This can be especially valuable for survivors who do not know a lot about investing or who may not be comfortable taking charge of financial assets. When I was an advisor, I had clients who were perfectly capable of taking care of their family's finances without my help, but retained me as an advisor so their surviving spouses would have someone to turn to. Some of these relationships continued for years, and I was pleased that I could help with their questions on many financial topics.

Your advisor can help you initiate the sometimes-awkward discussions you should have with your children, your parents, your spouse or other relatives concerning wills, healthcare issues and finances. These conversations can be extremely important, but too often they never happen because people don't know how to go about it.

Should you ever reach the point where your mental capacities are dwindling, your advisor should be able to protect your assets and your interests from anyone who might try to take advantage of you.

Many people wind up in divorce court, and if this happens to you, your advisor should be able to help you and your spouse gather information and evaluate various options. In some cases your advisor may recommend another advisor for either you or your spouse.

In fact, if you are ever unhappy with the work your advisor is doing for you, he should be willing to help you find somebody else who will work in your best interests. This may be painful for you and your advisor, but a truly great one will want you to be properly taken care of more than he wants to keep your business.

Your advisor may be able to give you access to certain exceptionally good mutual funds that are not available directly to the public. I'm thinking particularly of Dimensional Fund Advisors funds, which have many advantages over those you could buy on your own. These are the funds that I use in my own retirement portfolio.

Your advisor should always think about the tax implications of your portfolio and help you find ways to do what you need in the most tax-efficient manner.

Your advisor should help you determine a good benchmark against which to measure your investment performance and then provide quarterly returns showing your portfolio compared with the benchmark. Depending on your circumstances, this might include multiple benchmarks for various parts of your portfolio. He should review your performance with you at least annually.

Your advisor should determine when to rebalance your portfolio. This means tracking all of the assets in taxable and tax deferred portfolios and making the trades to keep the proper balance of stocks and bonds, as well as maintaining the proper balance of the many equity asset classes (large, small, value, growth, U.S. and international holdings).

When you retire, your advisor should help you choose the best pension and Social Security options.

Your advisor can help you determine if and when it makes sense to convert a traditional **IRA** to a **Roth IRA**. He can help you choose whether to contribute to a traditional account (either IRA or 401(k)) or a Roth account. He can help you determine when it is advantageous to combine various IRA accounts and when it makes sense to roll over a 401(k) from a former employer to a rollover IRA.

Your advisor should give you guidance on accounts he is not managing, including those in IRAs, 401(k) accounts and variable annuities. If you own company stock either within a 401(k) or separately, your advisor can help you determine whether to keep it or sell it. Some advisors charge for this service, while others don't.

Your advisor should be able to help you make decisions about stock options if you have them.

If you own illiquid investments such as raw land, rental properties or business contracts, your advisor should be able to help you figure out the best course of action.

If you have aging parents who don't have (or need) an advisor of their own, your advisor should help you advise them about the best ways to use and preserve their assets. When I was an advisor, I helped the parents of many clients move their money from certificates of deposit into better paying Vanguard bond funds. Sometimes this doubled or even tripled their cash flow with very little additional risk.

If your spouse is relatively uninvolved in your joint finances, a good advisor may be able to help him or her participate in making decisions. This is excellent background for the possibility that your previously uninterested spouse may outlive you.

When a new investment opportunity presents itself, your advisor can help you evaluate its prospects and risks and determine how it might – or might not – be right for you.

If you haven't already retired, your advisor can help you figure out whether your savings rate is likely to be adequate.

If you are contemplating an early retirement, your advisor should be able to make sure you have considered all the ramifications so that you go into retirement with the maximum probability of success.

He should help you decide which accounts to draw on for your retirement income and determine how much you can safely withdraw from your savings so you don't risk running out of money.

Your advisor can review the beneficiary designations on IRA and employee retirement accounts to make sure they reflect your wishes.

Your advisor can help you determine your need for life insurance and review your current coverage. He can do the same for disability insurance and long-term-care coverage.

Your advisor can review your charitable goals and help identify opportunities that might be especially tax-efficient.

If you are concerned about identity theft, your advisor can review ways to keep your information confidential.

Your advisor can "stress test" a retirement portfolio to determine how likely it will be able to last for a lifetime of varying investment returns and periodic withdrawals. This is one of the most important things you can get from an advisor, because once you have retired, running out of money is among the most significant risks that you face.

A good advisor can help couples negotiate their spending levels before and after retirement. Very often, one spouse is typically more of a spender while the other is more a saver. Over the years I helped many couples find solutions that preserved their financial viability and maintained the family peace.

When you need expert advice beyond what your advisor can give, he should be able to refer you to competent, reasonably priced professionals who can help you with legal matters, estate planning, insurance, banking and more.

Ideally, your advisor will be something of a psychologist who can help you and your spouse or partner prepare for – and get through – the inevitable difficult times in the market. It will be important to avoid making emotional choices, especially engaging in panic selling when the market is falling. Such decisions often prove to be very counterproductive.

Your advisor can help you choose the best options for setting aside money for education for your children or grandchildren.

Estate planning can get pretty complicated – and may require legal services – for investors with lots of money or unusual circumstances. Presumably your advisor is not an attorney, but he can still help you determine whether or not it's likely to be appropriate for you to use such things as family limited partnerships, irrevocable trusts, charitable remainder trusts or trusts to protect a disabled person.

When I look over this list, I realize it covers a great deal of territory. But these are all services that are readily available from many advisors.

In many cases, these services may be included at no extra cost. If that's the case, your financial advisor could wind up being one of the best bargains you'll ever find.

Chapter 10: **Getting the most from your advisor**

Getting the most from a broker

If your financial advisor is a broker, somebody who earns commissions by selling products, you will have to be especially vigilant to get the most benefit from this relationship.

Probably the very best way to use a broker is to invest only in exchange-traded funds (ETFs). These are legitimate products with low costs, high tax efficiency and minimal commissions for buying and selling. You can use ETFs to invest in all the major asset classes that I recommend. In short, you can get virtually everything you need with ETFs, and your broker can sell them to you. If you want to use my ETF recommendations please check them out at paulmerriman.com.

If you go beyond ETFs, then the following points should be your guide.

You should make sure you have done everything you can to protect yourself from being the victim of conflicts of interest, bad information and sales pressure. At a minimum, you should familiarize yourself with the contents of Book II. That way, you'll be able to recognize many of the ways some brokers take advantage of their clients.

Based on what's in those chapters, here are some ways you may be able to protect yourself. If you follow these suggestions, you are unlikely to wind up a victim of bad practices. What's more, you are likely to earn the respect of your broker, making him less likely to try to dupe you, and more likely to try to give you the full benefit of everything he knows.

Don't ever forget that your broker is a salesman.

Ask for objective evidence for any claims that your broker makes about performance, risks or past track records. A simple way to do this is to get in the habit of asking: "How do you know that?" You don't have to ask the question in a challenging or disbelieving way. Just ask it matter-of-factly. I think the results will be good, and if you ask that question at least once in every conversation with your broker, quite soon he will learn to be careful what he tells you.

If you buy load mutual funds, understand the differences between share classes (A, B and C). Get your broker to work out a set of assumptions and what you would pay with each share class. Then inquire about exchange-traded-fund alternatives and ask for the same analysis.

Ask your broker at least once a year for a report on the profitability of your entire account. If you can't get this, then keep your own records, using software such as Quicken if that makes it easier.

If there is any doubt in your mind, for any reason, about the wisdom of something your broker is recommending, don't act on it the same day.

If your broker offers to sell you something without a commission, don't take that recommendation until you understand how the broker will be paid.

When your broker makes a recommendation, ask him to talk about what could go wrong and how much money you could lose. If you act on the recommendation, keep a written record of what the broker told you. If you ever get into a dispute that goes to arbitration, your records could be invaluable to you.

If you don't have at least a basic understanding of how an investment is supposed to work, don't buy it. (If investors diligently followed this guideline, the complaints and grief involved in investing would go down dramatically.)

If your broker offers a suggestion for an investment that he says is likely to outperform the market – or a fixed-income investment that seems too good to be true – don't buy it until you get an objective professional second opinion.

Don't buy any initial public stock offering, no matter what. Study after study shows that, on average, IPOs underperform the stock market in their first year.

I know this can be hard, but you should always be alert for appeals to your emotions instead of facts. If your broker appears to be trying to stimulate your greed or your fear, treat this as a red flag.

Whenever your broker makes a recommendation, ask him if there's an alternative that costs less or involves less risk. If he says no, or if he tries to talk you out of such an alternative, make a written record of the conversation, just in case you someday wind up in arbitration or in court.

Don't let your broker talk you into ignoring the prospectus for a security he is recommending. Instead, ask him to go through it with you so you understand it. Pay particular attention to costs and risks and restrictions on when you can sell; if you can't sell it on any day you want to, then don't buy it.

Don't let your broker talk you out of getting a second opinion about his recommendations or discussing them with your spouse or partner before you commit.

Form a relationship with a CPA or somebody else who knows financial matters and who is not in competition with your broker. At least once a year, hire this person to review your brokerage activity and give you an objective opinion concerning the advice you are getting.

Getting the most from an hourly planner

If your financial advisor works for you by the hour, carefully pick and choose the assignments you give this person.

You'll have to start by knowing what you need, because you'll be balancing the benefits against the costs of every project or service you request. If you ask for everything this person can do for you, you could end up with a very big bill. If you severely restrict the scope of his work in order to save money, you could be, as they say, "penny wise and pound foolish."

Most hourly advisors will be happy to help you evaluate the potential benefit of each part of the work they could do for you. A good advisor will have enough other clients that he won't need to milk your account for the maximum number of billable hours.

Because this is an "a la carte" relationship, you can and should take things one step at a time, evaluating the quality of the service you get for each assignment before committing to the next one.

If you're not sure how to judge the quality of the work you're getting, hire a CPA or some other objective financial professional to review it with you. This will cost you something, but it's a good way to give yourself either peace of mind (knowing your advisor is doing work that other professionals respect) or a red flag (knowing the work is questionable in some way).

Even when you are paying by the hour, be sure to spend enough time to give your advisor all relevant facts and background. If you leave things out because you don't want to pay for an extra half hour of time, you can end up with flawed results. As they say in the computer industry, "garbage in, garbage out."

Getting the most from an asset-based advisor

If your financial advisor manages your assets and charges on that basis, then you will have a continuing relationship that isn't constrained by sales pressure or hourly billing. However, I believe you still have an obligation to use your advisor's time well, without wasting it. This will serve your interests anyway. Advisors are only human, and they usually have some control over whose calls they take right away and whose calls they postpone.

Perhaps the most important first step in getting the most from this relationship is for you to share all your personal financial information and be sure your advisor understands what you are concerned about.

As soon as you realize that something is bothering or worrying you, you should let your advisor know about it without waiting for a regularly scheduled meeting. Once your investments are properly allocated to meet your objectives, your concerns will more often be emotional than strictly financial. It's not a good idea to let something build up in your mind. You may hesitate to bother your advisor, but that will make it harder for him to do his job of taking care of you.

Respect your advisor's time. When I was an advisor, I sometimes would get a phone call from a client just before I had to go into a meeting, and I didn't have the time to fully explore the topic. I know this sometimes left clients thinking that I was not taking them seriously.

Unless something is urgent and needs immediate attention, start with an email that describes what you're concerned about. That will give your advisor time to think about the topic, check your records and do whatever research might help him address it for you. This way, he will be able to work for you at a convenient time when he can give it his full attention.

If you prefer your communications to be via email, let your advisor know that. If you'd rather talk on the phone, say so and tell your advisor the best times for you, such as early in the mornings or at noontime.

There will inevitably be times when you are exasperated for some reason, and you'll want to voice your complaint. How you go about doing that will have a significant effect on how (or whether) you get a satisfactory resolution. You are more likely to get what you want if you pay attention to your communication style.

Some clients have a knack for asking what they want in a way that makes their advisors want to accommodate them. Other clients seem to generate resistance and strife just by the way they say things.

One of my favorite clients was a soft-spoken retired insurance executive who had the nicest way of telling me he was unhappy. "Paul," he would say, "are you happy with the way things are going?" It was always easy for me to respond to this.

Another client took an opposite approach. I'd pick up the phone and hear: "Paul, you must be crazy!" I never took this personally, but it wasn't the best way this client could have opened a conversation.

Being the ideal client

Finally, and this applies no matter what type of advisor you have, I suggest you think about what you bring to the table in your relationship with your advisor. Your attitude and conduct will play a part in whether you get everything you should from your advisor.

Start by making sure you have realistic expectations. Your advisor can't control the market and can't know the future. He cannot eliminate unforeseen risks. He can't suddenly turn a losing investment into a profitable one. He can't eliminate your obligations to pay taxes if you owe them.

You won't get the maximum benefit from any advisor whom you distrust. So I recommend that you spend whatever time is necessary to choose an advisor who is worthy of your trust, and then give him that trust.

Your probability of success will be higher if you also have faith in the free-market system and in the future. Here's how I said it in my book *"Financial Fitness Forever"*: When you invest money, you must take a leap of faith. When you take that leap, you have to be confident that you'll have somewhere safe to land."

No matter how well you invest your money, the market will disappoint you from time to time. You should not treat your advisor as if he is to blame for what the market does, because he's not. Your advisor can counsel you and encourage you and help you learn whatever lessons you need to learn. You, however, are the only one who can supply the resilience and persistence needed to learn those lessons and keep going.

You'll get more from your advisor if you are patient than if you demand immediate results from every move you make. At one end of the spectrum (the wrong end to be on), there's the investor who buys a stock "as a long-term holding" and then decides to keep it or dump it depending on what happens to its price on the first day he owns it. At the other end of the spectrum, some investors are willing to wait for years before they judge the wisdom of today's decisions. This is a good topic for you to discuss sometime with your advisor.

No matter what type of investment advisor you work with, be sure to know your goals and have sensible plans for achieving them. If you and your advisor work together to set realistic objectives, and then routinely use those objectives as your compass, you will be getting what you should get.

BOOK II:
Get Screwed

BOOK II: **Forward**

The remaining chapters of this book describe many ways in which investors "Get Screwed" by brokers, brokerage firms, and the products they sell. As you read about sales pressures, conflicts of interest, shoddy products, shoddy ethics and bad information, you will have a negative impression. Perhaps your impression will be too negative.

If my job were to discuss most brokers as individual human beings, Book II would be very different. If you have a broker or know a broker, it's highly probable that you like him. He may be the sort of person you would want to count among your friends and neighbors. He probably treats his clients with courtesy and respect.

However, my job is to help you avoid Getting Screwed. To do that, you must understand that brokers do not – and in most cases cannot – work in isolation. They are part of a highly organized and very sophisticated industry that generates huge profits from individual clients. Even though many of those clients are unaware that those profits are reducing their financial future, they are stuck in a system that works against them.

In order to adequately describe that system, I have painted a picture using a very broad brush. Not every broker engages in the practices that I describe. But most brokers are subject to sales pressures and incentives that can easily lead to recommendations and actions that are not in the best interests of their clients.

If you have a good relationship with a broker, I'm not advocating a breakup or an end to the relationship. However, if you maintain that relationship, you should do so with your eyes wide open, and do your best to understand what is behind the recommendations and advice you are given.

The best way to do that is to educate yourself so you can recognize the behaviors and the products that may work against you. These chapters will give you that education.

As you read, remember that my criticism is not aimed at your broker as an individual. It's aimed at the system in which he has chosen to work and make a living.

Chapter 11: **Get screwed through sales pressure**

Pressure to generate sales is behind most of the bad experiences that clients have with brokers. In fact, it's safe to say that the sales commission is one of the primary drivers of the brokerage business.

I suspect most investors assume that commissions are an inescapable fact of life. But in the United Kingdom and Australia, effective January 1, 2013, it is illegal to sell commission-based financial advice. Financial advisors will have to charge for their services only by fees paid by their clients. In those countries, the brokerage business, as we know it in the United States, will no longer exist.

That may seem pretty radical. But think about what medical advice would be like if physicians earned a commission on every prescription they wrote for their patients? Does that seem like a good idea?

Keep this in mind as you read through this chapter, which lists **20 ways that investors Get Screwed** because of a corporate culture of pressure to make the sale.

1. In an article published at Wallstreetwarzone.com, Paul Farrell summed up the brokerage sales culture this way: "Over two thirds of securities are sold through brokers working on commission. These brokers are trained in aggressive tactics based on solid psychological principles that work against naïve, vulnerable investors."

Farrell cited "The 22 Keys to Sales Success: How to Make it Big in Financial Services," a book written by the president of an insurance company and the president of a non-degree school for people in business. This book, Farrell wrote, "is designed to turn a salesman into a pit bull who won't take 'no' for an answer" and who can "run circles around an unsuspecting sales prospect" by gaining psychological control over the sales transaction.

In order to make a sale and earn a commission, "A good line of bull is more important than information" about financial products, Farrell wrote. Successful selling requires the broker to find a way to overcome "the four fears that haunt every investor during every sales presentation."

Those four are the fear of making the wrong decision, the fear of what's unfamiliar, the fear of giving up control, and the fear of losing self-esteem.

In short, the broker must keep tight control of the situation while allowing the client to FEEL in control. This is deliberate psychological warfare, and the financial stakes for investors are high.

2. "Fraud" is a very strong word to use when describing the practices of brokers. But it's not really so far-fetched. Among the definitions of fraud is this: "something intended to deceive; deliberate trickery intended to gain an advantage."

Another definition focuses on "wrongful or criminal deception intended to result in financial or personal gain." I believe that explains what is behind a great deal of the investment advice and the practices of the typical broker.

The "criminal deception" is quite obvious in cases like Bernie Madoff and **Ponzi** himself.

We have become accustomed to deception in other sales arenas. For example we don't flinch when a car salesman says: "This is the best price I can offer you."

Most of us understand the role of the car salesman: to put us in new wheels any way he can. We're much less comfortable thinking that the person we trust with our financial affairs could be trying to deceive us. But deceit is a staple of the brokerage business.

The most common types of fraud would not exist if brokers and brokerage firms operated on a standard of fiduciary responsibility to their clients.

3. Boiler rooms. These are high-pressure sales operations in which salespeople make unsolicited phone calls to promote and sell securities, most often very cheap stocks that don't attract much attention otherwise.

These securities are usually unsuitable for investors who receive the calls, and sometimes they are outright fraudulent. The sales pitch is mostly made of half-truths and lies.

The name "boiler room" refers to a windowless, basement-level area of a building where many sales agents spend their time on the phones trying to generate business.

4. Many investors believe that discount brokerage houses don't have products to sell, and therefore these firms don't have salespeople motivated by sales commissions. Wrong.

In fact, many discount brokerages sell annuities and other products that pay big commissions. I once spoke with a broker at a large national discount brokerage firm who told me his bosses required annuities to make up a certain percentage of his new sales, even inside IRAs, where (as almost everybody in the industry understands) they have no business.

5. In Chapter 4 I referred to the practice of "churning" an account in order to generate purchases and sales – and the resulting income for a brokerage firm. If your broker (or his boss) decides your account has been too inactive to be profitable, you may get a call from your broker suggesting a review of all your investments. That sounds totally sensible, but there may be an ulterior motive behind the call.

Assume you own a stock that has performed poorly since you bought it, and you're understandably frustrated. Your broker may patiently go over your options with you. You can wait until the stock goes back up and you break even. Or you can look for a different stock that might make more money for you. (Which one of those options do you think your broker wants you to take? I bet you can figure that out pretty easily!)

At some point your broker may ask you, acting as if he has just thought of this, to imagine that you owned whatever amount of cash the stock is worth instead of owning the disappointing stock itself. He might ask: "Would you invest your cash in that company now, or would you want something with more potential for profit?"

Your broker knows what your answer will be, and he has just manipulated you into telling him what he wants to hear. And, miracle of miracles, that happens to be the very thing that your broker's bosses also want to come from your lips: Let's find something better.

Bingo, there's a sale and a purchase, each of which earns a commission for the brokerage firm. Worse, you will think your broker has just helped you do something smart, something that will make your financial future better. Actually, in all likelihood the exact opposite has happened.

Many academic studies have looked at what happens when an investor sells a "dog" stock and buys something else that's considered "hot." Historically, you have a better chance of making money by sticking with what you have than by selling it and buying something else.

If you stand pat, there's of course no guarantee that you will benefit. But if you sell the dog and buy something else, the broker is guaranteed to benefit.

In fact, a truly savvy investor might prefer to buy more shares of the disappointing stock while its price is low.

6. Brokers are often under pressure to sell new public stock offerings. A brokerage firm makes a commitment to sell some percentage of these offerings, and individual brokers are expected to unload the shares to clients. One reason for the pressure is to make sure the firm isn't left holding the bag after an initial offering drops, as was the case in the 2012 market debut of Facebook.

A friend who worked as a broker for a big national firm told me the following story about a public offering. The sales manager checked in with the broker to make sure he was selling his allotment. My friend made it clear he didn't like the stock and didn't intend to recommend it to his clients.

The sales manager calmly informed the broker that it was up to him. But if he didn't sell those shares, they were going into his own account – and of course he would have to pay for them.

In other words, "If you don't sell them, you own them." The broker quickly got the point, got on the phone and found clients willing to buy the shares allotted to him – shares that he didn't want to be stuck with himself.

7. Brokerage customers who are astute and observant may notice a cycle of the sales calls they get with "new ideas" for their money. Every broker is expected to generate a certain amount in commissions every month, and that often results in a big push to do business in the final days of the month.

One study concluded that many brokers produced two to five times as much in daily commissions in the final week of a month as they did earlier in the month.

Do you think all the best ideas just happen to emerge at the end of each month? Obviously, that is unlikely. What's very likely is that sales pressure is the culprit behind the end-of-the-month rush.

8. Brokers must meet annual sales goals. I once had a long (and to me, eye-opening) talk with a young broker who told me how the company tried to help him make his goals.

His quota required him to generate gross commissions for the firm of $120,000 a year. He said he thought of it as $10,000 a month. He was young and relatively new in the industry, so he decided to make relatively young people, mostly in their 30s and 40s, his target market.

The good news was that these people had money to invest regularly. The bad news was that this money should have been going into their 401(k) retirement plans. But there was a problem: If these people did what they should have, their investments wouldn't earn a dime in commissions for either the broker or the brokerage firm.

If this broker recommended the right things for these clients, he couldn't feed his own family. His bosses came to the rescue, giving him two options.

Option A: He could persuade his clients to put their regular savings into IRA accounts, which would be invested in load funds. If a client invested $400 a month in funds that paid a 5.75 percent commission, his firm would get only $276 a year. To reach his $120,000 annual quota, he would have to recruit more than 400 clients and keep every one of them investing $400 a month. That was an impossible task in the time he had available.

Option B: Instead, he could persuade his clients to invest $4,800 a year in variable universal life (VUL) insurance policies. Those products (very profitable to the insurance companies that issue them) often pay sales commissions equal to 50 percent of the first year's premium – or $2,400. In this scenario, he would have to recruit only 50 clients.

Though this seemed like a viable solution, it presented the broker with a very big problem. He knew that a VUL policy was an awful solution for his clients. He couldn't bring himself to foist this product on his clients, and he couldn't find another way to remain at the firm. So he left, much disillusioned with Wall Street.

9. The pressure to generate sales usually originates from the brokerage firm rather than from the broker. This plays out in the element of trust, which Wall Street relies on heavily.

You may be well aware that big brokerage firms have had ethical troubles, legal troubles and lawsuits. You may have concluded that the firm you use is not to be totally trusted. But you probably know and like your individual broker. You may even treat him like a friend of the family.

That trust is a precious commodity, and without it, Wall Street would collapse. After all, you aren't likely to buy or sell securities unless you trust the person making the recommendation.

However, as we have seen, your broker isn't always the person behind the recommendations you get. Your broker most likely reports to an office manager or a branch sales manager, who in turn may report to a regional or district manager. One step up the line is the national sales manager, who's so removed from the clients that he is not likely to care at all about you and your needs.

The national manager may be under pressure from the CEO, who has to answer to a board of directors. And the directors are (at least in theory) working for the owners of the company, usually public shareholders.

As a general rule, the farther up the ladder somebody is, the less he or she is likely to care about you. And unfortunately, that is the very person who wields the most power over what a broker is expected to recommend to you.

No matter how much you like and trust a broker who knows you, and may in fact care about you and your family, your broker has to answer to people who don't know you and don't have any reason to care about you except as a source of sales.

A similar situation exists in big banks. The people in a neighborhood branch know many of their customers and truly care about them. But the people downtown (or in New York City) don't know and don't really care. Unfortunately, they are the ones who make the rules that the employees in the branch must follow.

10. Sales are essential to running a brokerage firm, and they are not left to chance. Not on your life!

Securities salespeople, especially in their early years, are usually taught to work from a script. The first part of the script focuses on the reasons you should buy a certain product (the benefits). But the all-important part is training the salesperson to overcome your possible objections.

You can bet that the broker has been taught exactly how to deal with your complaints about the cost of commissions, the risks, and the need for liquidity.

You may insist that you need more time to study a prospectus or think about an important decision. The broker knows just what to say to persuade you to move now.

You may need to talk to your spouse. The broker knows just what to say to manipulate you into thinking you should assert your authority within your marriage.

You may need to get a second opinion from another advisor or professional. The broker knows just what to say to reestablish the fact that all your questions have been answered.

These scripts are practiced over and over until they become second nature. Salespeople are thoroughly trained in turning your "no" into a "yes."

The result is usually a sharp imbalance of power. When you combine a professional salesperson and a non-professional investor, the damage to the investor can add up quickly.

11. There's a big difference between a broker (salesperson) and a legitimate investment advisor. A great salesperson is one who generates lots of commissions. A great investment advisor, on the other hand, is one who knows the best ways to maximize your long-term financial success.

Unfortunately, it's easy to learn to trust a broker who's "a great guy" – a belief that makes you susceptible to believing things that you think you're paying the broker to protect you from!

What do you think makes a successful broker? What he knows? No! Who he knows? No! What club he belongs to? No! His golf handicap? No! Studies conclude that the most successful investment sales people are those who are most optimistic about the future.

Psychologists point to studies showing that people who are optimistic make better friends, make better parents – and make more money. But investors should remember that the optimist tends to see life through rose-colored glasses, and that can lead to overconfidence. Overly optimistic brokers can encourage investors to take more risks than they should. This is what happened big-time at the turn of the century with technology and Internet stocks.

12. Brokers themselves can fall for sales pitches. Some years ago, *Smart Money* magazine wrote an article about what happens in brokerage firms after a mutual fund wholesaler visits a city. (Of course I'm talking about funds that pay sales commissions.)

The wholesaler is paid handsomely to persuade brokers to sell the funds that he represents, usually all from a single fund family. During a visit, the wholesaler typically takes brokers to lunch or dinner or invites them to a special event, perhaps with expensive reserved seats. Now ask yourself this question: If the funds this person represents were top-notch, would the fund family need to spend that kind of money drumming up sales? Of course not.

The free lunch and expensive sports tickets may be good for the brokers. But are they good for the clients? I don't think so, especially if they lead the broker to sell mediocre funds to unsuspecting clients. Unfortunately, that's exactly the result that the *Smart Money* article described.

Recently I had breakfast with an investor whose advice comes from a broker who's a long-time friend and member of his church. This was all he needed to know to give his trust to this friend.

At breakfast, I learned that a big chunk of my friend's portfolio was invested in the Oppenheimer Champion Income Fund. This bond fund has very high expenses (1.36 percent per year) and for 10 years it lost more than 7% annually. Why did my friend own it? Most likely the reason is that the broker who sold it to him earned a 4.75% commission, which is unusually high for a bond fund.

There was nothing at all about this fund that made it worth recommending to a client (or a fellow church member). In fact, the broker could have earned a similar commission on a bond fund with a better track record. So why was the Oppenheimer fund the one that the client bought? My best guess is that this sale happened soon after the Oppenheimer wholesaler came through town.

13. Many brokers believe their experience makes them immune to such sales pitches. They may proudly say (as some have said to me): "I refuse to go to those sales meetings because all they want us to do is sell something that will make money for the firm. Those meetings are for the newbies."

Given the sales culture in brokerage firms, it is highly plausible that younger and less experienced brokers will be under strong pressure to attend the sales meetings in order to help them make their quotas.

The problem for you as a client is that you never know, when you hear a convincing sales pitch for a stock or a fund manager, the source of that pitch. But if your broker is relatively new, you can be pretty sure that what you are hearing sounds a lot like what he and his fellow brokers heard at a sales meeting.

14. Risk is arguably the most important characteristic of any investment you may be thinking of making. But if a broker acknowledges the risk that is inherent in an investment, that gets in the way of sales. So risks are minimized.

The salesperson knows you're likely to be scared off by thinking about the reality that you could lose money, and you may balk instead of buy.

During the great technology stock bubble of the late 1990s, many investors decided that risk was an out-of-date concept that no longer applied when there was so much easy money to be made. Everyone in the investment industry knows how easy it is to lose 50 percent, or even 100 percent, in a booming technology stock.

But very few brokers told the clients that, and the clients didn't want to hear it. As a result, many fortunes were lost and many lives changed for the worse.

15. When you "go home to think it over" after hearing a sales pitch for a product, that time for reflection gets in the way of sales. Accordingly it is discouraged, even though any truly valid idea should stand up well to extra scrutiny.

A former broker told me that very early in his career a sales manager routinely observed him in order to help him become a better salesman. The manager overheard the young broker tell a couple, after a long meeting filled with suggestions, to go home and talk it over, then call him the next day.

Afterwards, the manager was livid, calling the broker into his office. "Don't you ever suggest that somebody go home and think about it," he said. "If they insist on that, OK; but I don't want you to ever suggest it."

16. If you are an educated investor – or if you show a great curiosity about the facts, your knowledge gets in the way of sales.

A salesman can sell based on facts, which is hard. The client can always need further facts or need more time to understand the facts. Alternatively, a salesman can sell based on emotions. Once you are hooked emotionally, you are unlikely to ask too many questions and will probably stay hooked.

The easy path to a sale is a brief pitch that focuses on the benefits of the product. Possible problems and probable risks are "inconvenient" and are therefore skimmed over very lightly, or ignored altogether.

If you know and truly understand all the facts, you may be a threat to Wall Street's profits.

17. Government regulations require brokers to give clients, in writing, a detailed description of many investments, including its costs and risks. But in order to keep a sale from going south, a broker will discourage clients from reading that material, which is known as a prospectus.

Brokers sometimes behave as if the prospectus is their biggest enemy. I once attended a luncheon hosted by a financial planning organization, with a guest speaker whose presentation was called "My 101 Best Sales Ideas." (Note that the purpose of the luncheon was not to educate Wall Street's front-line people about product features. No, it was designed to help them manipulate clients into buying securities.)

The speaker didn't give all 101 tips, which were contained in a book he was happy to sell. Many of the tips he did give were, in my view, blatantly unethical.

For example, one of his points focused on how to get the prospectus – that pesky but required legal document – out of the client's sight. That way the client wouldn't get too interested in the risks he would be taking.

The speaker suggested the broker shrug off the prospectus as a formality prepared by and for attorneys. He suggested referring to attorneys lightheartedly as the firm's "sales prevention department."

"You might even remark," he told his eager audience of brokers, "that if we all let the attorneys have their way, nothing good would ever happen." There was laughter from his audience.

At this point we were instructed to read a paragraph of text that had been left on our tables. I picked up one of the copies and read it. It was a relatively complex paragraph of legalese that nobody would want to read. The speaker suggested the broker hand this paragraph to a prospect or client and ask the person to identify what it was.

Like everybody else in the audience, I failed to recognize it until the speaker revealed that it was The Lord's Prayer written by an attorney. The whole room broke out in laughter at this, giving the speaker the opening to say: "That laughter you just heard is what you'll hear from your client. And when you hear it, you know it's time for you to simply reach over, close the prospectus and get on with your sales presentation."

18. In the spring of 2012, *AARP Magazine* published an article by Allan Roth, a fee-only certified financial planner, CPA and author, in which he spoke of the financial industry's "perverse incentives and self-serving ethical standards."

The article is worth quoting from, because it gives an insider's view. Here's an example of a statement with which I agree: "By and large, we're good people, which is why we can be so convincing – and so potentially dangerous to your money." Conflict of interest, Roth wrote, "pervades everything we do."

Here are two more quotes that illustrate his plain talk: "Bad advice is epidemic in my industry." ... "We make money by getting it from you."

To succeed, brokers must win our confidence. "We spend a great deal of effort trying to win your trust," Roth wrote. At least 100 professional designations are available to planners, "each meant to convey expertise in something. Some prove only that the planner passed an easy exam."

Roth said he was once contacted by the owners of a Web site that offered to designate him as being among the top 1 percent of U.S. financial advisors if he would pay an annual fee of hundreds of dollars.

Another time, the Consumers Research Council of America (check out this link if you want to know more) offered to designate Roth as one of "America's Top Financial Planners" and send him a certificate and a plaque with that designation if he would pay a $183 fee.

Roth paid the fee. When he was asked what name he wanted on the certificate, he submitted Max Tailwagger, the name of his dog. Max, as a result, was designated by this organization as one of the best planners in the country.

Remember this the next time your broker flashes a fancy designation that suggests he is one of the best. If you want, ask him what he had to do in order to receive the designation. Better yet, just look elsewhere for advice and help.

19. Impressive titles (always capitalized) like Vice President and Wealth Management Specialist are meaningless from the client's point of view. Brokerage firms usually hand out vice president titles purely on the basis of how much money a broker generates in commissions.

The titles can induce clients to think they are dealing with one of the best brokers. The problem is that, in this case, "the best" only means the most effective in separating clients from their money.

20. Some selling pressures are motivated by what brokers know about the cycle of their business. Investors do not want to invest when the market is going down. Intellectually, most investors understand it's better to buy when prices are depressed, but our financial decisions are mostly controlled by our emotions.

On the other hand, most investors find it amazingly easy to invest when the market is high, even though that means the risk of loss is greater.

All these crazy emotional decisions have taught brokers that they must make their money when people will invest, when the market is high. If they have been through an extended bear market they know how their income can suffer – maybe down by more than 50% from the good times.

This reality motivates brokers to sell very hard when the market is up – and when risk is up – and to save some money for the inevitable bad times ahead. Most of them understand that this works against their clients, but it's simply a fact of life in the brokerage business.

Chapter 12: **Get screwed through conflicts of interest**

When you pay somebody for financial advice, you are probably depending heavily on that person's knowledge, experience, judgment and competence. You may quite naturally expect that your trusted advisor, who after all is being paid, will look out for your interests.

A broker who accepts commissions for selling you products has a built-in conflict of interest. In fact, brokers' interests and their clients' interests are very often in conflict. What's best for one may not be good at all for the other. In this chapter I'll show you **9 examples of how conflict of interest happens**:

1. I was once called to testify as an expert witness when a broker had been sued for selling inappropriate investments to a widow who had collected on a life insurance policy. She had made it very clear to the broker that she expected to need the insurance proceeds to pay debts in the following year. In other words, she had a real short-term need for this money.

The correct advice would be to put the money into something totally riskless and highly liquid, so she could get that money right away when she needed it. A money-market fund would have been a reasonable solution.

However, that would not have been profitable to the broker or the firm he worked for. Instead, he recommended that she invest in risky, high-commission products that seriously jeopardized her ability to get her money when she needed it. The brokerage firm had covered itself legally by giving her a prospectus (a legal document outlining risks, fees and other information), knowing that she was unlikely to read it. Like most clients, this woman relied on what she was told by the broker.

I was asked to testify on behalf of the client, and the brokerage firm hired another expert witness to present its side of the case. After the trial, in private, I asked this other expert: "Why do you really think the broker sold her these products instead of keeping the money liquid to meet her needs?"

I've never forgotten his answer: "If he had recommended that she put the money into something completely liquid, he ran the risk that another salesperson would figure out how to sell something to her, and then that person would get the commission. If he doesn't get the commission, probably somebody else will."

2. Commissions are structured in a way that can lead brokers to do the exact opposite of what's best for clients. Commissions are highest on the products that are the most difficult to sell. Those are the products that relatively few people want or need. And what ARE those products? They are complex, risky investments that often make it hard to get your money back when you need it without paying a penalty of some sort.

Because of these high commissions on bad products, brokers often find themselves caught in an ethical trap. The very things that will make them the most money (and maybe win expense-paid trips to warm exotic locales in winter) are the ones that require the biggest moral compromises because they are not likely to be appropriate for the client.

Life insurance provides a simple example: Most fee-only advisors recommend term life insurance policies, which have relatively low costs and pay relatively low commissions. These are good for clients who need life insurance. By contrast, salespeople who are paid on commission tend to favor whole life policies. Whole life policies are much more profitable for insurance companies, which pay high commissions to the people who sell them. But whole life insurance is much less advantageous for clients.

How big are the differences? For a given level of insurance, a whole life policy can cost 10 times as much as a term life policy. A broker who sells a term policy may get a commission of 20 percent of the first year's premium. But the commission on a whole life policy may be 100 percent of the first year's premium.

Think about what this means to a broker. If he sells you a term policy with a first-year premium of $300, he might get a commission of $60. If he sells you the same amount of whole life, with a first-year premium of $3,000, he might get a commission of $3,000, or 50 times more than the product that is likely to be a better solution for the client.

Which policy do you think the broker will want to sell?

3. Despite the high commissions they may pay, brokerage customers aren't likely to get their brokers' top-priority attention when they need it the most. If you do not have more money to invest, your broker will be inclined – and incentivized – to spend his time finding the next client (which means the next commission). This isn't personal; it's just the way the sales business works.

During extended or severe bear markets, brokers have to work much harder – and spend much more time – to bring in new business. This may be just the time that existing clients need help. Unfortunately, it can be the time they are least likely to get that help.

4. Older people can be easy targets for slick salespeople, and the brokerage industry knows how to cash in on this fact. Experts believe that the No. 1 crime against elderly people is none other than investment fraud.

Retired people often have substantial assets, making their accounts potentially much more lucrative for brokers than the accounts of younger people who are saving and investing regularly.

Older people often trust too much and are too willing to "follow the herd" and do what their friends are doing. Too many times, their grown children, who could protect them, are too busy or live too far away. This creates a profitable playground for the unscrupulous salesman.

It's estimated that every year, investment fraud affects 7.3 million older people in the United States. That estimate is based on incidents that are reported. The real number is probably much higher, since people – especially older people – are reluctant to have their friends and families know they have been duped.

Here's a link to an article that illuminates this point: www.seniorsite.com/finance/financial-scams-expected-to-boom-as-boomers-age.asp

5. In a much-publicized case in Seattle some years back, a Merrill Lynch broker was used to making more than $500,000 a year and leading a lavish lifestyle. She was hailed by Merrill Lynch as its top-producing female salesperson and was held up as a model for her peers.

The broker, Molly Carol Wilson, was known as a tireless worker, not afraid to make 100 or more cold calls a day. But some of her clients complained to regulatory agencies that she made excessive trades in their accounts in order to generate commissions. They said the trades cost them hundreds of thousands of dollars.

Merrill Lynch later paid more than $430,000 to three of Wilson's former clients to compensate them for excessive trading activity and recommending unsuitable securities.

Wilson's branch manager at Merrill Lynch had signed off on every trade she initiated for her clients. Because she earned so much money for the firm, the manager was willing to overlook some of her actions. However, lawsuits and complaints (and publicity) piled up, and Wilson was eventually fired from Merrill Lynch.

Shortly thereafter, Wilson started her own securities firm to work independently. Within a year, she was in hot water with securities regulators.

She was charged with taking $280,000 directly from the accounts of four elderly clients (including all three of those who were later compensated $430,000 by Merrill Lynch for her actions while she was there). Regulators said Wilson used these clients' money to pay her own living expenses, including payments on the Rolls Royce she drove.

Regulators finally shut down her business, and she was sentenced to 75 months in the Washington State Corrections Center for Women near Tacoma.

6. Hoping to win the confidence of clients, many brokerage houses infuse their brokers with puffed-up credentials that are mostly meaningless. Sometimes they tell outright lies, though rarely in writing.

Upon learning that someone is a "financial planner," a prospective client may assume a level of expertise. But often, all that's required to legally call yourself a financial planner is to file some registration forms with your state's securities regulators.

One common lie is the statement (or the carefully crafted implication) that a broker is a Certified Financial Planner, a prestigious designation that can be obtained only by rigorous education and years of experience.

According to one study, only about one out of five "financial planners" is a Certified Financial Planner. Many would-be CFPs have fulfilled only some of the requirements for that designation, but they still represent themselves to the public as Certified Financial Planners.

7. Some years ago, an insurance company approached me, wanting to develop a variable annuity that would be based on our firm's investment management. I listened carefully to the presentation, thinking this might be a way to create a variable annuity that would actually be beneficial for clients.

But after hearing the details, I told the company representative that all the high costs built into this product would make it a poor choice for investors. In response, he assured me that that wouldn't be a problem: "If you put a big enough commission on something, the salespeople will sell anything." We passed on the opportunity.

8. I recently spoke with a woman who followed the advice of her broker to buy a tax-exempt bond fund (which paid the broker a commission, naturally). The broker made her feel as if she were doing a very smart thing by avoiding taxes.

I know of at least three reasons this was an awful recommendation.

- First, tax-exempt bonds almost always pay less interest than taxable ones. Because of that, they are suitable only for investors in the highest tax brackets. In the case I've just described, this woman's tax bracket was relatively low, and she would have earned more, even after taxes, by investing in taxable bonds.

- Second, almost immediately she began withdrawing money from the bond fund in order to meet her cash flow needs. This meant her broker earned a commission on money that she should not have invested in the first place, some of which remained in the bond fund for only a few weeks. At a very minimum, the broker should have made sure that at least a full year's worth of her cash needs was safely in a bank account or a money-market fund.

- Third, even if she had left all the money in the bond fund, the interest rate on the bonds was so low (and it's even lower now) that she would not have been able to recover the cost of the commission for more than three years.

9. Brokers sometimes offer stocks and funds on a "commission-free" basis. Clients think they are getting a special deal, but usually the exact opposite is true: They are paying more than they normally would.

In one case with which I am familiar, a closed-end fund, called Colonial High Income Trust, made an initial public offering through various brokerage firms, including Raymond James.

The Raymond James firm gave its brokers an "internal use only" memo urging them to persuade clients, especially retirees, to buy the initial shares before they began trading on the stock exchange. The memo said brokers would get a commission of 45 cents for every share they sold that way.

The memo suggested that the brokers, in their sales pitches, emphasize that there would be **no commission** to pay on the shares if they were bought before trading started, contrasting that with the commission they would have to pay if they waited to buy.

This was pure deception. Because the 45-cent commission was built into the initial price of the shares, it didn't have to be disclosed. After the shares started trading, buyers would have to pay a disclosed commission, which would have been much less than 45 cents per share.

One broker told clients that this was a safe product with no commission. In fact, neither of those statements was true.

Chapter 13: Get screwed by unethical practices

Shady or non-existent ethics are unfortunately common in the brokerage business. In this chapter, I'll give you **eight examples that illustrate some of the most important issues:**

1. In order to win your confidence and your business, your broker must have your trust. And nothing erodes trust as fast as a lack of credibility.

Yet your broker can be his own worst enemy. When he tells you, "This is the best solution for your situation" and it clearly is not, he is demonstrating either incompetence or a lack of ethics – or both. When he says "This is what I do with my own money," and you are pretty sure that is untrue, your trust is probably on its way out the door.

I believe most brokers engage in unethical practices. It's not that they are trying to cheat people, but they have painted themselves into a corner. In order to make a living, they must sell products that are designed to produce mediocre returns for investors (along with high fees for Wall Street).

Even a competent, knowledgeable and experienced broker gets caught in this ethical trap. So I ask you, what good are knowledge, competence and experience if they cannot be exercised for your benefit?

2. Brokers owe their allegiance not to you but to the firm for which they work. Even though he wants you to believe it's just the opposite, your broker must put the firm's interests ahead of his own – and ahead of yours as well.

In plain English, if your broker wants to keep his job, any conflict between what's best for you and what's best for the firm must be resolved in favor of the firm.

I've talked to many former brokers who lost their jobs for failing to produce enough commission income from their clients. In most cases, they told me, their commissions suffered because they were trying to do the right thing for their clients. The sad part is they loved being able to help people with their finances; they just wanted to do it ethically.

3. One of the worst things brokers do to their clients is follow the herd, doing what everybody else seems to be doing. They do this even though they understand that the exact opposite – buying when most people want to sell, selling when most people want to buy – is what produces favorable long-term returns.

I attribute this to some combination of incompetence, unethical practices and just plain old laziness. It's so much easier to identify what everybody else is doing. It's so much easier to persuade clients to do what everybody else is doing. And it's so easy to hide behind the veil of conventional wisdom and "common sense."

As a result, brokers' clients often end up not with thoughtful strategies but with collections of individual "good ideas" that were easy to sell (and easy for the clients to buy) at the time. Brokers know it's always harder to educate an investor than to make a sale.

4. In many cases, brokers don't get adequate oversight from their firms or from regulators. The first line of defense against many abuses is the broker's branch manager, who typically sees (and approves) the paperwork for every trade.

The manager probably doesn't know the clients personally, and he's under corporate pressure to produce commission income. His main worry about questionable trading is likely to be the possibility of legal troubles. As a result, abuse of clients' trust and money is unlikely to grab his attention unless it's so egregious that regulators could become interested.

A branch manager may find it convenient not to look too deeply into the sales practices of any broker who is a big producer.

ıge houses do have to deal with serious legal troubles and their customers. A simple Internet search for the name of any d the word "complaints" will probably yield an afternoon's worth ...ɔant reading.

If you have the time, do another search substituting the word "fraud" for "complaints." I did that with one of the largest brokerage firms and got 1.8 million results. For another firm, that search turned up almost seven million results. Those are firms I would never want to entrust my money to, even if I had the most personable broker in the world.

Most clients never know about this side of the brokerage business. If you are walking in the door of a brokerage office for the first time, you may have no clue that the firm could have a long history of unhappy clients or has paid hundreds of millions of dollars in fines and legal settlements.

Even if you never have any cause to complain or file a lawsuit, the commissions and other costs you pay must cover the legal expenses of the firm. In other words, you're paying for illegal and unethical sales practices even if they don't affect you directly.

6. FINRA, the Financial Industry Regulatory Authority Inc., a private corporation (not a government agency), is the successor to the National Association of Securities Dealers. It has the power to censure brokers, but not necessarily put them out of business.

In a case involving what I regard as blatant fraud, FINRA cited a broker in Tyler, Texas, for selling high-risk products to clients who should not have bought them and who would not have done so if they had understood them.

The products in this case were Direxion exchange-traded funds (ETFs), some of which engaged in short selling. Half of this broker's clients traded these securities on margin, even though many of them weren't aware that they were borrowing money to make the purchases. Some of the investors were as old as 91, and some had incomes as low as $25,000.

The agency quoted the Direxion prospectus (the legal document that brokers hope clients won't read) as saying that the Direxion funds were suitable only for investors who understood the risks of leverage, daily trading and short selling.

This same broker was disciplined by FINRA for excessive trading in clients' accounts. The agency said one client's trades generated $9,600 in commissions in an account with an average monthly balance of $17,000. I know that most readers will never believe they could end up working with such an awful broker. But many of them do.

7. When brokers are looking for trusting clients, nothing is sacred. Literally.

In the spring of 2012, the Securities and Exchange Commission, a federal agency with strong enforcement power, charged City Capital Corp. and two of its former executives, with running an $11 million Ponzi scheme aimed at socially conscious, church-going investors.

One of those charged was Ephren Taylor, 29 years old. He managed to get himself introduced to conservative congregations across the country as somebody who had made lots of money as a teenager.

Liberally quoting scriptures, he promised that he could do the same for his fellow Christians. He disappeared after lawsuits were filed by investors; mostly African-Americans, in 40 states.

Some of the plaintiffs had invested their life savings, expecting returns of 20 percent, only to find that there was nothing behind the promises and the perpetrators were nowhere to be found. The SEC claims most of the money went to pay for Taylor's lavish lifestyle.

The core of the operation, like that of any Ponzi scheme, was using money from new investors to make payments to previous ones. As long as lots of new money comes in the door, the scheme continues. But if new money dries up, the house of cards can collapse quickly.

8. Many sales pitches rely on bald-face lies in order to work. Many brokers are experts at knowing how to lie effectively – and profitably. A *Wall Street Journal* article on the subject of lying reported that the practice normally begins in children at the age of 2.

More than a third of 3-year-olds will lie in order to escape trouble, and more than half of children from 4 to 7 will lie to stay out of trouble or to get attention and approval.

The article cited studies showing that parents can detect only 53 percent of the fibs that their preschool kids tell. By the time they're 9 to 11, the article said, children can often fool their parents three times out of four.

So, here's a question for you to think about: If we assume that kids are amateur liars and they're that good, how are those same parents able to cope with the professionally motivated lies of their brokers?

Not well. After all, moms and dads want to believe their kids, just as they want to believe their brokers.

Chapter 14: **Get screwed by bad information**

In dozens of ways, maybe even hundreds, brokers dispense bad information to their clients. This ranges from outright lies to innuendoes to misrepresentations to partial truths. This does not happen by accident. The patterns I am about to describe are carefully scripted to persuade clients and potential clients to do things that will make money for brokers and the firms they work for.

Some of these practices are subtle and hard to notice; others are fairly blatant. In this chapter, I have given **16 examples of how this happens**:

1. In many cases, what your broker neglects to tell you may be more important than what he actually tells you. For example, you probably won't be told that the extra expense of most broker-sold products has an enormous long-term effect on your portfolio.

For example, if you are paying an extra 1 percent on a mutual fund, they may minimize the extra 1% yearly cost as a mere $100 per $10,000 that you invest. Agreed, $100 isn't going to change your financial future. But as I pointed out in my book, FIRST-TIME INVESTOR: Grow & Protect Your Money, an additional 1 percent annual cost (reducing your return by 1 percent) can make a difference of hundreds of thousands, or even millions, of dollars over your investing lifetime.

This seemingly small difference can literally take away half of the total lifetime money you have available to spend and/or to leave to your heirs. This is absolutely crucial information. But your broker won't tell you.

2. Almost always, your broker will focus on what he thinks you want to hear, instead of what you need to know. An old adage in the brokerage business is that most investors want three things: First, they want income; then they want more income; and third they want even more income.

The higher the income that's expected from a product, the easier it is to sell. In the late 1980s, high-yield bonds were paying 16% and more. Brokers made a lot of money selling these, and why would clients resist?

High-yield bonds were known in the trade as "junk bonds," and for good reason. They carried such high risks that the only way companies could sell them was by offering unusually high interest rates to compensate for all that risk.

In 1990, some high-yield bond funds lost as much as 40 percent of their value. Investors didn't see this coming, but their brokers could have warned them. That didn't happen, because the warning would have prevented the sale – and thus prevented the all-important commission.

3. Sales commissions on mutual funds are totally optional. Any good financial professional can help a client choose no-load funds and fill out the easy paperwork. But brokers make those sales commissions sound like a necessary part of the process.

A common pitch for the load or sales commission goes something like this: "There is no free lunch. Those no-load funds are getting their money from you one way or another. We all need to be paid for what we do."

This is a very convenient lie to tell an unsuspecting client who does not know better! The truth is that there are two types of expenses that investors must pay in all mutual funds: operational expenses and marketing expenses.

But when you buy a load fund, the fund company pays your brokerage firm a commission of 4 to 6 percent of whatever you invest. That means that of the money you think you are investing, actually only 94 to 96 cents of every dollar actually goes to work for you. You suffer an immediate loss on the day you open an account, a loss you can never recover. The entire "benefit" of that sales charge belongs exclusively to Wall Street.

No free lunch? You are the one who provides the lunch, and your broker is the one who gets to eat it.

4. Meaningless, misleading statistics are a staple of Wall Street's sales pitch. A good example is the **Morningstar** rating system, which ranks mutual funds from one (worst) to five (best) stars.

Most people naturally want to invest in winners instead of losers. Accordingly, brokers and the marketing departments of mutual fund families eagerly capitalize on any fund with a five-star rating from Morningstar.

The implication is that Morningstar has somehow determined that a five-star fund is likely to outperform in the future. In fact, the rating system is based entirely on past performance, a notoriously unreliable indicator of future performance. Brokers, brokerage firms and mutual fund companies certainly understand this.

Your broker will never tell you about the many rigorous studies that have been unable to determine any predictive value in Morningstar's ratings. I'll tell you about one, a study made by Vanguard in 2009, covering these ratings going back to 1990.

Vanguard wanted to know how likely it was that a mutual fund would outperform its benchmark in the 36 months after it received a five-star rating. After studying hundreds of ratings over hundreds of periods, Vanguard concluded that a five-star fund had a 39 percent probability (about four chances in 10) of outperforming its benchmark after it achieved the favorable rating.

More surprising yet is that Vanguard also found that funds with one-star ratings (supposedly the worst) had a higher probability – 46 percent – of outperforming their benchmarks.

In other words, the "worst" did better than the "best." Furthermore, neither group had even a 50-50 chance of outperforming its benchmark. This is very important information for mutual fund investors. But they are not likely to learn it from their brokers.

5. Brokers are very adept at making misleading comparisons sound plausible. Over the past 80 years, value funds (ones that own relatively unpopular stocks) have outperformed the Standard & Poor's 500 Index by one to four percentage points annually. This makes it easy for a broker to find a value fund and compare it favorably to "the market."

If he successfully persuades you to buy the value fund, and if that fund outperforms the S&P 500 Index after you buy it, you may conclude that your broker is a wiz at recognizing the best funds. But all that's really happening is he is taking advantage of your unfamiliarity with asset classes.

Value funds invest in a different asset class (value stocks) than the S&P 500 Index (a blend of value and growth stocks). Everybody in the investment industry understands that they are apples and oranges. Similarly, anybody who knows the first thing about cars understands that a Corvette has a higher top speed than a Toyota Camry. The Corvette isn't necessarily better than the Camry; the two cars are designed to achieve different things.

You can instantly recognize the difference between a sports car and a family sedan. But if you don't know the difference between asset classes, you can come to believe that your broker is a genius when in fact he is just telling you what is easily predictable.

6. The misinformation you get may be blatantly misleading and carefully chosen to lead you to a certain conclusion. In one case, a broker for a large national firm bragged to clients that his recommendations had outperformed the **S&P 500 Index** over a 10-year period. That sounds impressive, especially when the broker was recommending stocks from the S&P 500 Index's own portfolio.

But the broker didn't mention a very crucial fact: He was using a published return for the index that did not include the effect of dividends. Dividends typically make up 40 percent or more, over long periods, of the total return of the Standard & Poor's 500 Index.

The return of the broker's recommendations included dividends, of course, making it extremely easy for his stock picks to "outperform." If he had disclosed the difference, clients would have recognized it instantly.

A stove with five working burners will put out more heat than a similar stove with only three, and anybody can figure that out quickly. But if the number of burners was hidden and all you saw was the total heat output, you could be forgiven for concluding that one stove was much better than the other.

7. Brokers know that people who invest in stocks and stock funds are more interested in performance than in just about everything else. And performance comes in so many varieties that there's always something that looks hot that can be sold to generate a commission.

Short-term bursts of good (and bad, for that matter) performance are legion in the stock market. This gives brokers plenty of material to capture the imagination (and the dollars) of eager clients.

What the broker doesn't reveal is that short-term performance is essentially meaningless in predicting future long-term performance – which is what the clients want and need.

Even a full decade of performance can be a misleading predictor. In the 1990s, there was no bear market, and many investors concluded that they could abandon caution and move full speed into the future with technology stocks.

Unfortunately, in the 2000-2002 technology bust, the Standard & Poor's 500 Index lost 49.1 percent. A few years later the index lost 56.8 percent in the 2007-2009 meltdown. These two severe bear markets ruined many a fortune and many a future that had been built on the optimism of looking at recent short-term performance.

8. Brokers like to present themselves as experts at choosing investment managers. It's an appealing idea. What's not to like about having your own personal guide to "the best of the best" among all the professionals out there? And after all, it does seem logical that your broker has the time and the resources to perform this role.

The broker's hand-picked recommendations among mutual funds can seem like a winning strategy. Invariably, you will find that these recommendations have good recent performance, making them "winners."

However, your broker won't tell you about the numerous studies that have failed to find any conclusive connection between recent performance and future performance.

Your broker may show how he has chosen the best funds from several fund families. This might seem to be one more indicator of your broker's expertise and hard work on your behalf. But in fact, using multiple families of load funds could be a clever gambit by the broker to generate more commission income.

If you have $1 million to invest and you put it all in a single fund family, the overall percentage load is usually reduced substantially based on the number of dollars. This is a "fee break" that fund companies give in order to attract large investors, and every broker is thoroughly familiar with this. Sometimes a load goes as low as 0.25 percent for investments of $1 million or more.

But if your broker can persuade you to divide your $1 million among several fund families, he has cleverly deprived you of the volume discount you could otherwise get, while generating higher income from commissions.

Worse, your broker will make this seem like it's in your best interest because you are getting "the very best hand-picked expertise" from multiple fund families.

9. Brokers often conveniently neglect to put their sales pitches in a context that would make them meaningful and help clients make good choices. If your broker can get you to invest in the Templeton Developing Market Fund, you may pay a sales commission up to 5.75 percent. This shouldn't be a difficult sale, since this fund, run by famed manager Mark Mobius, had an annual compound return of 11.9 percent for the 10 years ended June 30, 2012.

This should be a no-brainer, right? Who wouldn't want that performance during a decade when most investments struggled just to keep up with inflation? Who wouldn't want the expertise of a manager who could do that well over 10 full years?

In making this sales pitch, your broker might not tell you that in that same period, the Vanguard Emerging Markets Index Fund compounded at 13.7 percent. And that fund has no sales commission. If your broker was really trying to find you the best emerging markets investment, why wouldn't he recommend the fund that in 10 years turned a $10,000 investment into $36,108 (Vanguard) instead of the one that turned $10,000 into only $29,012 (Templeton)? See my next point?

10. A commission that seems small can actually become huge.

The paperwork on the sale of the Templeton emerging markets fund might disclose a commission of $575, and you might think that's what it cost you to follow the broker's advice.

But that $575 never had the chance to work for you, and the remaining $9,425 earned nearly two percentage points less in return. The net result is that your true cost of following a broker's advice, in retrospect, would have been $7,096, the difference between what you could have made at Vanguard and what you would have actually made at Templeton.

The reason your money went into Templeton instead of Vanguard was the commission. On a $10,000 investment, your real cost could be calculated as a 71 percent commission ($7,096) instead of a 5.75 percent commission ($575).

If the broker were really working for you, he would also point out that the Vanguard fund has lower internal trading costs (turnover) and considerably more diversification, making it less risky. He would finish with the reality that these differences are not just something from the past but variables that are likely to persist as long as you hold the fund.

11. Brokers claim, incorrectly, that their research departments can beat the market. If that were the case, brokerage firms' mutual funds should have top performance. But they don't. Vanguard founder John Bogle reports that Fidelity Investments made a study of broker-managed funds from 1994 through 2003.

In this 10-year period, funds managed by brokerage firms had worse performance than those managed by banks, financial conglomerates, and mutual fund companies. For example, Merrill Lynch funds achieved 18 fewer percentage points of return than the industry average for comparable funds. Morgan Stanley funds were nine percentage points below average, and those of Wells Fargo and Smith Barney were eight percentage points behind.

12. A recent study by Schwab Institutional found that 75 percent of investors' actual portfolios were not suitable for the people who owned them, given their financial situations and their objectives.

This has to result from some combination of poor information, sales pressure and lack of knowledge – often on the part of both the investor and the salesperson. While much of this may result from poor choices by investors, brokers are obviously not adequately "protecting" their clients adequately from themselves.

13. A recent study by CEG Worldwide concluded that more than 94 percent of the financial advisors who held themselves out to be "wealth managers" were more focused on product sales than managing financial issues for clients.

The problem here is that the title "wealth manager" is rich with implied promises. It sounds sophisticated and impressive. Unfortunately, too many people are willing to focus on the trappings. A wolf in sheep's clothing is still a wolf.

If you work with a broker, you want one who is knowledgeable and who understands the business of investing beyond what he is likely to pick up during sales training. But in many cases, this is asking a great deal, especially of young brokers.

This prompts me to mention that if you are a first-time investor and you're starting a relationship with a brokerage firm, you're likely to be assigned to a young broker who's trying hard to build enough business to keep his job. You're much less likely to have a seasoned broker with a couple decades or more of experience.

Young brokers are highly unlikely to be familiar with the nuances and the importance of things like expenses, portfolio turnover, tax efficiency and asset class selection. If there is something important to the future of my investments, I want my financial advisor to know it. It's not enough that they have "heard about the concept," as one broker said to me when he was describing his knowledge of asset class selection.

I recall talking to another young broker who admitted he didn't really understand the difference between using index funds and using actively managed funds, despite the fact that he worked for a large national brokerage firm.

14. Brokers can talk about all the wonderful things they've done for clients, but they don't have verifiable track records. If you ask to see a broker's track record, you may be told that it's impossible to define because everybody's needs are different.

More likely, you'll be told the track record of whatever that broker is recommending at the moment. Any novice can easily put together a list of investments that have outstanding recent performance. However, many rigorous academic studies have found over and over that recent past performance is a very poor predictor of future performance.

If you want to avoid being misled, you'll think about this until you understand it. For example, assume your broker is recommending a group of mutual funds, saying they appreciated at 20 percent a year for the past decade.

That may be a truthful track record. But it's not the track record of your broker unless he was recommending that exact group of funds 10 years ago, before the 20 percent per year performance. Almost certainly you will find that that is not the case.

15. The following point may seem ironic, but it's true: Many financial salespeople have very little background or experience in business and financial markets. When I was hired by a big Wall Street firm in 1966, the office manager made it clear that understanding investments was not the important part of my job. The most important part was being a persistent salesman. He told me that being a successful Fuller Brush salesman would be a good background for the business I was getting into.

The firm told me what to sell, and I didn't have to know all the things that our clients expected me to know. Because of that, many of those clients didn't get the expertise or help they had a right to receive in return for the sales commissions and other fees they paid.

Common sense dictates that you shouldn't pay for something you don't get. When you pay an unnecessary sales commission, you should at the very least get some thoughtful and knowledgeable financial planning and guidance. But you're not likely to get it from a broker.

16. Brokers, especially young ones, may give lip service to diversification, but many of them refuse to let this concept get in the way of making commissions and pumping up their own egos.

Many brokers have the idea they can play the market with their clients' money, and they often hold themselves out as security analysts who can pick stocks. Because of this overconfidence, they believe their clients don't need many stocks in a portfolio; they often say 15 or 20 is plenty, and you can be pretty sure that their picks will be concentrated in asset classes with hot recent performance.

These brokers either don't know about, or choose to ignore, the large body of academic research that concludes that adequate diversification requires at least 100 to 200 stocks in every major asset class.

It's not hard to see why this research is so inconvenient to stock-picking brokers: No broker could keep up with all those companies, and no ordinary client could buy them all.

A stock-picking broker's clients may believe they have an expert working for them. But that "expert" is unlikely to tell those clients that year after year, independent academic studies have reached the same two conclusions:

- Portfolios of 20 stocks are much riskier than portfolios of 100 stocks.
- There's no evidence that a 20-stock portfolio is likely to provide higher performance than a 100-stock one.

Chapter 15: **Get screwed by bad products**

Unfortunately, the majority of financial products are designed primarily to make money for the people who manage them and sell them. If the buyer makes money, that's fine; but that is much less important.

I think there's a category of products that could be called unethical because of their unnecessarily high expenses, high commissions, and the misleading ways they are sold. The combined impact of these "design flaws" can easily cost investors one percent or more in annual return, enough, as we have seen, to totally change an investor's long-term financial future.

When you work with a broker, you are likely to be offered the chance to buy many really bad products. **Here, in no particular order, are 17 examples:**

1. Proprietary products – things that you can't get anywhere else – should raise red flags. We all know that competition is a desirable way to keep costs under control and an incentive to produce quality products.

But many brokers and insurance salespeople represent products from only one fund family or one insurance company. Financial advisors at banks tend to steer their customers' investments into the bank's brand of products. Often, a bank or a brokerage house will sell funds that are identical to those customers can actually get elsewhere for far less.

My son, Jeff Merriman-Cohen, wrote an article focused on a simple but important question: "Whose name is on the door?" If the door on an advisor's office has the name of XYZ Brokers, you immediately know who pays the bills, who is in charge, and who tells the broker what he can and cannot sell.

The exact same dynamic is in effect at banks and insurance companies.

When your broker can choose among thousands of products, he can pick the very best one for you – even though that doesn't necessarily happen. But when his inventory is very limited, your broker can't do that, and you're likely to wind up with an inferior product and inferior results.

2. Many brokers and others who sell financial products actually know very little about investing; they may do financial advising only part-time. A principal at a financial services company once told me his firm handled investment products only as a way to get access to clients with the potential to buy really big insurance policies.

A banker whose job was selling investment products told me he was supposed to focus on annuities, which pay relatively high commissions, and he also sold stock and bond funds occasionally as well. I asked if the bank had taught him about the merits of index funds, and he admitted the bank never did. So much for putting the customer's interest first.

3. Brokers and insurance salesmen can make a lot of money selling products that do a poor job of taking care of the people who buy them. One awful example is the index annuity.

If you are a broker and you want a million-dollar paycheck, you could spend all your time selling index annuities, which pay very high commissions.

Why are these products so bad? For one thing, their expenses are very high for what little value they deliver. For another, they tie up investors' money, making it very expensive to liquidate an investment in its early years. For a third, they are so complex that, sometimes, even attorneys can't figure out the contracts that investors are asked to sign.

I have spoken to dozens of investors who bought index annuities. Almost to a person, they have told me they never would have done so if they understood what they were getting into.

Brokers like index annuities because they can use the magic word "guarantee" as part of the sales pitch. Never mind that what's actually guaranteed may be watered down so much that it's a joke.

If your broker is trying to sell you an index annuity, I doubt you will ever be told one very relevant fact: A relatively simple portfolio of mutual funds, split equally between stock funds and bond funds, has historically produced better returns than the all-equity index annuity. And the mutual fund portfolio has done that with less risk, greater probability of success, greater liquidity and more tax efficiency.

4. One thing that makes a product "bad" for investors is lack of **liquidity**. That means you can't get your money out quickly without jumping through some hoops or paying a penalty. Imagine a bank CD that goes for 10 years and could cost you up to 10 percent of your money if you need it back sooner.

If you think that's extreme, it's not. In some illiquid products, in order to get your money quickly you may have no choice except to sell on the open market. If there are buyers, you may be looking at offers to pay you only 50 cents on the dollar – if you're lucky. The reason is that there aren't any brokers pushing those products any more. Brokers get paid very well for selling "new" products but not much for selling "used" ones.

It can be extremely disheartening to learn the hard, cold fact that the product about which you and your broker were once so excited is now regarded as something of a dog.

When you're considering an illiquid investment, the prospectus (that legal document your broker wants you to ignore) will clearly identify lack of liquidity as a risk. But your broker will make it seem like the product is in great demand ("I have only a limited inventory left in this, so don't wait too long!").

I was once a victim of this deception myself when I invested in a limited partnership. The salesman told me he could certainly find a buyer for my partnership interest if I wanted out.

I had fully intended to stay with the investment for the long term, but then the circumstances in my life changed. I needed the money. Guess what: The salesman was unable to find a buyer who was willing to pay more than pennies on the dollar. The main thing I gained from this investment was a very painful and costly lesson about the importance of liquidity.

5. Many brokerage firms hold an inventory of securities that they expect to sell at a higher-than-normal profit margin – usually because they carry above-average risks.

The firms take some risk while they hold onto these products, so they hope to sell them quickly. For example, when the market for adjustable rate preferred securities started to dry up, some brokerage firms realized they were about to be stuck owning securities that nobody wanted.

What did those firms do?

- Did they suck it up and take their medicine like grownups by selling at depressed market prices? Sorry, no.
- Did they sell the products at reduced prices the way Nordstrom might try to unload clothes that were out of fashion? Sorry, no.
- Did they quickly call as many clients as possible telling them about a "great deal" they could buy "with no commission?" YES!

The brokerage firms were "generously" giving up potential sales commissions; in return. When these high-risk securities later experienced huge losses, those losses were borne by the customers, not the brokerage firms.

6. Fad products are usually bad products. When some segment of the investment world is hot, many brokerage firms and mutual fund companies are eager to jump on the bandwagon.

In 1999 and 2000, as the technology-stock bubble was at its peak and even after it started to burst, Merrill Lynch introduced some Internet/technology funds. For example, a manager was hired to start a "focus" fund with 20 of his favorite technology stocks. Another new fund focused on internet companies. These funds seemed like a great idea to the marketing department, and within a few days, $2 billion was raised.

Merrill Lynch made a lot of money very fast. But within two years, the funds' portfolios had lost about 80 percent of their value.

I don't fault a mutual fund company for offering high-risk funds. But I believe Merrill Lynch understood the potential for 80 percent losses. When that level of risk is not disclosed except in the fine print of a prospectus, then in my book the fund becomes an awful product.

Fortunately, this is a bad product that's easy to protect yourself from. Don't invest in something unless it has a meaningfully long track record and you understand the losses that previous investors experienced.

7. By now you know that I think actively managed funds are usually "bad" products for most investors. But Wall Street has a seemingly endless arsenal of arguments in favor of them.

For example, when a client expresses the desire to own a low-cost index fund, a broker has no trouble admitting that such a fund will include all the "winning" stocks in an asset class.

But, he will add, the index fund also includes all the rotten apples in that asset class, stocks that will be a drag on the performance of the good ones. Why not hire a smart manager, he will ask, who can weed out the bad ones so you own only the good ones?

This seems to make a lot of sense, but in real life it just hasn't ever been done consistently and reliably. (Otherwise all investors would soon become very wealthy.)

In fact, the committee at Standard & Poor's Corp. that's in charge of its famous 500-stock index, has tried to do this very thing. From time to time they weed out underperformers and add companies that seem more promising for one reason or another.

Time after time, the academic researchers have come to the same conclusion: The S&P 500 committee would have been better off leaving the index alone.

8. The non-traded real estate investment trust (REIT) is a recent addition to the Really Bad Products Hall of Fame. InvestmentNews.com reported that over seven years, the eight largest non-traded REITs just barely broke even, assuming all dividends had been reinvested.

However, investors typically buy these securities for their income. Investors who lived off their dividends, instead of reinvesting them, saw the value of their REITs drop by 37 percent. (During the same period, Vanguard's REIT mutual fund appreciated by more than 50 percent, assuming investors reinvested the dividends.)That's just lousy performance, of course, not enough by itself to qualify an investment for membership in the (imaginary) Hall of Fame. Two things make this a really rotten product. First, it paid sales commissions of 7 to 15 percent. Second, it was marketed heavily to seniors as substitutes for bonds (on which the commissions are typically 1 percent) and certificates of deposit (which have even lower commissions or none at all).

Most people buy bonds and CDs for their relative safety in comparison with stocks. In doing so, they willingly accept the lower expected returns of bonds. But brokers know that even conservative investors still want higher returns. Some unscrupulous brokers offer REITs along with a promise (never in writing, of course) that "everything will be fine."

Everything, of course, is not "fine," since many non-traded REITs have filed for bankruptcy. One broker held seminars in which he told unsophisticated investors that these securities were "bonds on steroids," totally ignoring their high risks. In some cases he charged buyers a 7 percent commission on these illiquid REITs and added an annual 1.9 percent "wealth management" fee.

9. The variable annuity is a very profitable product for the insurance companies that produce it and the salespeople who induce investors to buy it. But almost always it is a poor investment choice. It is a bad product, overpriced and overhyped – and subject to harsh tax consequences.

Brokers often invoke the magic word "guarantee" to make the point that investors "can't lose" in a variable annuity. I think this is a total fabrication. Here's how it works:

You invest $100,000 in a variable annuity, and the insurance company promises that if you die, your heirs will receive at least $100,000, regardless of what happened to the investments in the annuity portfolio.

However, if you want to leave $100,000 to your heirs, there are much better ways to do it. You can buy life insurance for much less money than an upfront payment to an insurance company of $100,000.

If you want to provide future income for yourself, you have much better choices. However, if your broker thinks he can get you to buy a variable annuity, he may never tell you about those better choices.

10. When you get bad information about a bad product, it's a lethal combination. A variable annuity is a bad product. Here's a bad sales pitch for it.

The pitch promises tax-deferred growth. That's true, but it ignores the fact that the same benefit is available a lot of other ways without the high expenses, mandatory (and usually overpriced) insurance, lack of liquidity, high commissions, limited investment options and harsh tax treatment.

If what you need is tax-deferred growth, you can get it without the high costs of an annuity through an IRA or a 401(k). You can even get it in a taxable account if you buy and hold ETFs or tax-managed mutual funds.

11. Here's another bad sales pitch for the same bad product: You don't have to pay a sales charge when you buy a variable annuity, so all your money goes to work for you, unlike mutual funds with loads and ETFs with brokerage commissions.

This is technically correct. The money you pay for an annuity goes into the annuity. But the broker gets a commission, usually 5 to 7 percent of what you have invested. You don't pay it upfront, but you pay unnecessarily high expenses (up to 2.5 percent more than no-load index funds charge) and the commission comes out of the unnecessary expense that you pay.

This is the reason for the "early surrender" charges levied on annuity owners who want their money back in the first five to 10 years. Once you no longer own the annuity, the insurance company can't charge you for that out-of-sight commission. Hence, you get hit with an exit fee.

12. This no-sales-commission pitch also shows up when brokers are trying to sell Class B shares in mutual funds. It's true that these have no up-front, visible commission, and they are sometimes described to investors (unethically and illegally) as commission-free.

However, class B shares carry higher expenses that result in lower returns when compared with Class A shares (which charge an up-front commission).

And just like variable annuities, Class B mutual fund shares carry an early-redemption penalty that gradually decreases over time.

13. Insurance companies like to take business away from one another, and the so-called "bonus annuity" has become a popular weapon in that war. It may be good for salespeople, but it's not necessarily good for investors.

If you already own a variable annuity, you may be reluctant to replace it with a new one because you'll have to pay a surrender charge in order to sell the one you own. Enter the bonus annuity, designed to make you believe you are getting something for nothing.

If you buy this product, the insurance company may offer to add a "bonus" equal to 7 to 10 percent of the money you invested. This may more than make up for any surrender charge you paid.

But the bonus is hardly free money. You may have to wait years to withdraw it from your account. You may be able to get it only by annuitizing the entire contract, thus giving up the right to ever collect your principal.

Worse, bonus annuities typically charge higher annual fees, pay less interest and impose higher surrender charges than non-bonus annuities. Unfortunately, most people who buy these products remain happily ignorant.

14. Another bad pitch for this same bad product: As mentioned earlier, when you buy a variable annuity you get a guaranteed death benefit.

The guarantee states that if the owner dies, the value of the account will never be less than the owner invested. Sounds pretty good, right? But if you think insurance companies are going to hand out free lunches, think again. If you read the contract carefully (which very few people ever do), you are likely to learn that this "benefit" is discontinued when you reach a certain age. And it's likely to disappear if you choose to turn this "annuity" into a REAL annuity by taking lifetime payments.

Further, the insurance company regards this "benefit" as life insurance, and you'll be charged for it even after your account value is well above the initial "guaranteed" value.

In fact, it's even worse than that: If you invest $100,000 and after a few years your account triples in value to $300,000, the insurance company has virtually no risk of having to pay out a "death benefit." But it continues to charge for the insurance, and the charge, based on the current value of the account, has tripled.

So you are being charged three times as much for something that you're much less likely to ever collect. From the point of view of the insurance company, this is brilliant. From your point of view, it is a white-collar form of highway robbery.

15. Still another bad pitch that brokers make when they are selling this bad product is that you can get a lifetime stream of income that guarantees you will never run out of money no matter how long you live.

This is called annuitizing the contract. When you choose to do this, you give up the right to the underlying value of the account. You can't get your initial investment back, and you can't leave it to your heirs.

When you annuitize, the insurance company guarantees to pay you a monthly income that will not run out during your lifetime. The amount will depend on your age, the value of the account, and the settlement option you choose.

There's nothing wrong with this option, but if this is what you want and need, you may be able to get a much better deal elsewhere.

Brokers who are eager to sell you an annuity will often use two contradictory sales pitches for the product. They will tell you that you'll be able to build up an estate with taxes deferred. And they'll tell you about the guaranteed income for life.

It sounds like a fabulous combination, and you may think you've finally done something very smart to secure your family's future. The problem is that you can't have both those benefits. If you choose the monthly payments, you can't leave the contract to your heirs. If you want to leave the contract in your will, you can't annuitize it.

You can have chocolate. Or you can have vanilla. But you can't have both.

16. Here's an even worse feature of the variable annuity: You may not actually have the choice between chocolate and vanilla. Some contracts are written so that when the buyer reaches a certain age, the monthly-payment option automatically kicks in.

If you were thinking of leaving the value of this product to your heirs and you didn't know of this provision until you reached the age of conversion, your estate planning could be frustrated in a big way.

Your broker may or may not mention this to you.

17. Brokers like the commissions from variable annuities so much that they'll sometimes persuade clients to roll over money from a 401(k) or similar retirement plan into an IRA, then buy an annuity within the IRA.

This is legal, but in my opinion it should not be. The pitch is that the client can continue to benefit from tax-deferred growth and "get the safety of the guaranteed death benefit." We've already seen that this "benefit" helps the insurance company more often than it helps people who buy annuities.

Buying an annuity within an IRA violates one of the cardinal rules of sound financial planning. The high commissions and high expenses of variable annuities are often explained away as the necessary costs of getting tax-deferred growth.

But if your assets are in an IRA, then they already get tax-deferred growth. Converting those assets to a variable annuity simply adds excess expenses and fees without giving you any meaningful benefit.

Chapter 16: **Get screwed by emotional appeals**

Any successful salesperson learns early that buying decisions are much more often made on the basis of emotions than on the basis of logic and reason. Securities salespeople have devised many ways, some of them pretty sneaky and sleazy, to manipulate investors into doing things that will make money for the sales force, but not necessarily for the investor.

It won't surprise you to know that brokers' training includes the notion that investors "buy the sizzle, not the steak." Your broker doesn't want to bore you with lots of facts about a company, its products and its competition. He wants to get you excited – and thus in a buying mood.

Salespeople know that we human beings are hard-wired in a way that leads our intellectual functions to quickly give way when our emotions kick in. This, Wall Street knows, is the level on which most financial decisions are made.

In this chapter, I'll give you **11 examples that may help you recognize when this could be happening to you or somebody you care about**:

1. Brokers want and need clients who will be loyal to them, and the industry knows just where to start: family and friends. Imagine that you're a young broker and you have just completed your training and have your license. Now you can begin to sell. Almost certainly your first assignment will be signing up your friends and family members as clients. These are the people who will be most likely to give you their trust, to want to help you get started.

It sounds lovely on the surface. But it's filled with danger for the friends and family members. Every young broker is bound to make mistakes. If you're the broker, do you want to make those errors with your friends' money and your family's money? If you are a friend or family member, do you want to take this risk?

Virtually every good financial expert I know believes people should be extremely cautious about loaning money to friends and relatives. I believe the same caution should apply to taking the advice of a brand-new broker – even if he's a friend or family member.

2. Your broker has been taught that he will be more successful if you think of him as your friend. You'll naturally be greeted with a smile whenever you meet, and you'll be treated as an important person. This is standard for sales of all types. There's always an ulterior motive, and most of us have learned to expect that from salespeople.

Chances are high that your broker will want to get to know about you, your family, your work, your favorite activities, your beliefs, your aspirations and so forth. Sometimes you might get a call that's carefully designed to make you think your broker's friendship is genuine.

One broker told me: "I make a point of calling clients once in a while just to check in and see how they're doing without making any sales pitch. That way they'll learn that I'm not always calling to sell them something. That makes it more likely they will take my call when I need to sell them something."

3. You might be shocked to learn what your broker *really* thinks of you. Privately, many brokers regard themselves as vastly superior to their clients – and often they openly use derogatory terms to describe the very people they work so hard to butter up.

The book described by Paul Farrell urges salespeople to remember that they are the professionals and their clients are just amateurs. The message is this: Don't let the amateurs take over the sales process.

Wall Street Journal columnist Jason Zweig once published a list of some of the terms he had heard brokers use to describe their clients. The list includes: chumps, suckers, marks, targets, victims, dupes, baby seals, guppies, pigeons, geese, ducks (as in "when the ducks quack, feed 'em"), cattle, sheep, and lambs to be shorn.

Your broker may treat you as a very important and intelligent individual. But once you walk out the door or hang up the phone, he might use some of those words to describe you as he brags to his colleagues about what he persuaded you to do.

The result is that your broker is pretending to have a relationship with you that is false. If you heard his private conversations about you, any trust you had in the broker could vanish in a heartbeat.

4. In an earlier chapter I spoke about my experience getting taken in by the notion that Jack Sikma, who was then a celebrity in my hometown, was investing in a certain product. I loved the fantasy of thinking I was doing what Jack was doing. The reality was all together different.

If a broker can't hook you with an emotional appeal based on a celebrity, maybe a great story will do the trick, since investors love to own stocks with appealing stories. "Story stocks" are typically those of companies that are developing some hot new product or line of business (think of a new smartphone or tablet computer, for example). Often the company itself is very new, giving investors "a chance to get in on the ground floor."

These appeals are easy to make, because investors invariably hope they can ride the wave of "the next Apple" or "the next Google."

Peter Lynch, the legendary former manager of Fidelity's giant Magellan Fund, once said he had never made any money on a story stock. If he can't do it, what makes individuals think they can? I think the answer is that hope springs eternal.

I hate to throw too much cold water on your hopes and dreams, but you need to know how Wall Street really works.

If the story about a company is true, and it's about to launch the next dynamite product or service, that fact will be well known. In-the-know investors will probably have already made their bets. On the other hand, if the story isn't true, how are you supposed to find that out? And does "the story" adequately include the things that could go terribly wrong?

In 2012, millions of investors were star struck by Facebook, which raised an unprecedented amount of money in its initial public stock offering. A few months later, the company's stock had lost nearly half its value.

5. Brokers would quickly go broke if they were completely honest and told you the unvarnished and complete truth about a stock they are recommending. To do that, your broker might have to say something like this: "I am recommending this because I believe the price is likely to go up.

"However, many other people have known about this stock for some time, and they have had the opportunity to buy it for less than its current price. In fact, some of those early investors are trying to sell right now to lock in their gains.

"Today's price reflects everything that millions of smart investors know about the company. Although I'm very high on this stock, it's impossible to know the future of this or any other company. Many people think this company has a wonderful future ahead of it. Others think it's not likely to do much for investors. Still others think it is headed for big trouble. That's how the markets work. There's just no way to know the future."

Would that be an effective sales pitch? Hardly!

6. If stories and celebrities aren't enough to spur a client into action, there's always urgency – or the false sense of urgency.

This urgency may be built on the notion of scarcity. If you are a broker and your firm has only 1,000 shares left of some hot initial public stock offering (available to clients without paying the usual sales commission), your client can't afford to dawdle over the decision. It's easy to train a broker to say: "If you want to get in on this deal, you'd better make your decision now."

This implies that the stock in question is "certain" to be worth a lot more in the near future. Unfortunately, that "certainty" is always a myth. That's why it's never put in writing.

7. Brokers sometimes get us to override our common sense by appealing to our vanity. They know that we want to think of ourselves as smarter than average. After all, we have picked a smarter-than-average broker, and we've beaten the averages by saving some money that's available for investment. What's more, our broker treats us as if we are special. So why should we settle for an investment that is just average?

This is a good sales pitch for your broker to use when he wants to sell you actively managed mutual funds, those with managers who have a strategy for beating the market. It doesn't matter that dozens of academic studies reveal that relatively few active managers actually beat the market. Nor does it matter that those funds have above-average expenses and above-average turnover (trading) costs that you pay regardless of whether the manager is a success or a failure.

Your broker may tell you that passively managed index funds will force you – obviously somebody who is "above average" – to settle for only average returns. In fact this is a subtle lie that most brokerage clients find easy to accept.

Index funds capture the return of an asset class, for example the Standard & Poor's 500 Index, without trying to beat that return. That's accepting the market, but it's not the average return.

Average would represent the actual returns of all investors in a particular asset class. The majority of investors underperform the asset class (index) because of expenses and mistakes of active management – and of course because of the tendency of investors to make emotionally-based decisions about when to buy and when to sell.

As a result, the average investor winds up with much lower returns than those of index funds of comparable levels of risk. Here's what that means: If you invest in an index fund, you are virtually guaranteed to get an above-average return. If you buy an actively managed fund, your return is very likely to be below average.

Your broker certainly understands this, but he'll never tell you. That might make you feel gloomy instead of cheerful, and it would get in the way of making the sale.

8. Impatience is one of the biggest enemies of investment success. But brokers need this very impatience in order to keep generating sales. I'm convinced that long-term investment success results from finding a good strategy, then patiently sticking to it over a long period.

Think of the difference in mentality between a hunter and a farmer. A hunter is somebody who ventures into the unfamiliar world looking for opportunity that can be captured. The hunter loves the excitement of the chase and is willing to take the risks that go along with it. The problem, of course, is that when you go hunting, really bad things can happen.
A farmer, on the other hand, is somebody who is content to plant a field of crops, carefully tend that field and then patiently wait for nature to take its course.

Brokers prefer clients who think like hunters, clients who want quick results and crave emotional stimulation. Wall Street makes a ton of money from clients like these.

A registered investment advisor, by contrast, has much more of the mentality of a farmer. His professional life isn't nearly as exciting as that of a broker. And his pay is likely to be lower than that of a high-producing broker.

9. Some brokerage operations are known as "pump and dump" shops or "bucket" shops. They are designed specifically to prey on unsuspecting investors who are willing to believe that it's "easier" for a stock price to go from 10 cents to $1 than it is for the price to go from $1 to $10 or from $10 to $100. Their offerings tend to appeal the investors looking for quick, easy wealth.

"Pump-and-dump" brokers know that we like to be treated as big shots, and that we will feel much more important if we own 100,000 shares than if we own only 100. The inescapable truth is that 100,000 shares that sell for two cents each are worth exactly the same as 100 shares selling for $20 each.

But, I have run into many people over the years who seem to love to be able to brag that they own 100,000 shares of some company. It makes them seem like big hitters. Brokers take advantage of this by selling them very cheap stocks.

These are known in the industry as "penny stocks." They are usually associated with extreme get-rich-quick hopes and stories. And they usually are beneficial only to the professionals who sell them and who sometimes earn commissions or markups as high as 50 percent.

10. A broker who wants to keep your business knows he needs to provide peace of mind. Feigned friendship is one way to provide it. Another is creating a false sense of security.

When an investor's portfolio is doing poorly in a declining market, the broker is likely to say, "You're doing fine. Don't worry about it. Your investments are worth a lot more than they're selling for. You just have to be patient."

That is a message that all investment clients like to hear. But coming from a broker, that message might really mean something like: "I know you are losing money, and I am worried that you will panic and take your business somewhere else. Please, please, please just stick with me for awhile and, if we are lucky, maybe things will improve enough that I'll be able to sell you some more things."

11. Brokers themselves are sometimes duped by product salespeople, and even the firms they work for. In June 2012, Allen Stanford was sentenced to 110 years in prison for a $7 billion scheme that lasted over two decades and involved fake bank certificates of deposit.

Stanford owned a broker/dealer firm (which had 31 U.S. offices) that sold the CDs, promising interest of two to four percentage points higher than what was available at real banks. Naturally, these were very easy to sell, and the firm raised a lot of money.

The brokers who did the selling didn't have a clue that most of the money they raised was going straight to Stanford himself to fund his lavish lifestyle. They didn't have a clue that anything at all was fishy, even though any fifth-grader might have asked where the extra 4 percent return was going to come from.

Most investors in these fake CDs lost their money, and they got no help from their brokers, who earned huge commissions selling these phony products and who fought vigorously in court to avoid having to give those commissions back.

This illustrates one of my favorite quotes from John Bogle: "It's amazing how difficult it is for a man to understand something if he's paid a small fortune not to understand it."

BOOK II: **Afterward**

If you have made it all the way through Book II, you are, unfortunately, likely to either disbelieve what I've written or come away with feelings of disgust and distrust of the brokerage industry.

As I wrote in the Forward to these last six chapters, my intention is to educate you so that you can make informed, smart decisions about whom you hire to help you with your investments.

To be a successful investor, you have to place your trust in people, in products, and in the future. This entire book has been focused on the people part of that equation.

My final advice is simple. Trust, but trust warily, knowingly and carefully. In these pages, you have the tools to do that, and I wish you nothing but success.

Your comments and questions are welcome at: http://www.PaulMerriman.com

About: **The Authors**

Paul Merriman

Paul Merriman is nationally recognized as an authority on mutual funds, index investing, asset allocation and both buy-and-hold and active management strategies.

He was the founder of Paul A. Merriman & Associates, an investment advisory firm that is now Merriman LLC. The Seattle-based firm manages more than $1.5 billion for more than 2,000 households throughout the United States.

In his retirement, Paul remains passionately committed to educating and empowering investors. The **"How To Invest" series** distills his decades of expertise into concise investment books targeted to specific audiences and investor interests.

Paul is also the author of four previous books on personal investing, including ***Financial Fitness Forever: 5 Steps To More Money, Less Risk and More Peace of Mind*** (McGraw Hill, Oct. 2011). The book was part of the "Financial Fitness Kit" offered on the TV show, "Financial Fitness After 50" that Paul created exclusively to raise funds for local Public Broadcasting Service (PBS) stations. The kit also included a workbook, six CDs and five DVDs.

Paul's book, ***Live It Up Without Outliving Your Money! Creating The Perfect Retirement***, published by John Wiley & Sons, was released in an updated edition June 2008.

Over the years Paul has led more than 1,000 investor workshops, hosted a weekly radio program and has been a featured guest on local, regional and national television shows. Paul has written many articles for FundAdvice.com, a service of Merriman LLC. This Web site was identified by *Forbes* as one of the best online resources for investors.

Paul's weekly podcast, "**Sound Investing**," was named by *Money* magazine as the best money podcast in 2008. Paul has been widely quoted in national publications and has spoken to many local chapters of the American Association of Individual Investors (AAII). Twice he has been a featured guest speaker at Harvard University's investor psychology conference.

Paul began his career in the 1960s, working briefly as a broker for a major Wall Street firm. He concluded that Wall Street was burdened with too many conflicts of interest and decided to help small companies raise venture capital. In 1979, he became president and chairman of a public manufacturing company in the Pacific Northwest. He retired in 1982 to create his independent investment management firm.

Paul is the recipient of a distinguished alumni award from Western Washington University's School of Economics and is a founding member of the board of directors of Global HELP, a Seattle-based non-profit organization that produces medical publications and distributes them for free or at low cost to doctors and other health care workers in developing nations.

Paul donates all profits from Regalo LLC to Global-Help and a scholarship fund at Western Washington University.

For questions and comments, email: PM@PaulMerriman.com

Richard Buck

Richard Buck was a Seattle Times business reporter for 20 years, capping a 30-year journalism career that included eight years as a writer and editor for The Associated Press. He began working with Paul in 1993 and retired in the fall of 2011 as senior editor of Merriman Inc. In that position he helped Paul and other Merriman staff members write many articles and was the ghostwriter for Paul's previous books, ***Financial Fitness Forever*** and ***Live It Up Without Outliving Your Money!*** in addition to the ***How To Invest Series***.

Richard has also chosen to receive no compensation and to donate all profits from the sale of this series to a scholarship fund at his alma mater, Willamette University.

29140698R00066

Made in the USA
Lexington, KY
15 January 2014